Protest

Protest

A Cultural Introduction to Social Movements

James M. Jasper

polity

First published in 2014 by Polity Press
Reprinted 2015 (twice), 2016

Polity Press
65 Bridge Street
Cambridge CB2 1UR, UK

Polity Press
350 Main Street
Malden, MA 02148, USA

ISBN-13: 978-0-7456-5516-1
ISBN-13: 978-0-7456-5517-8(pb)

A catalogue record for this book is available from the British Library.

Typeset in 11 on 13 pt Sabon by
Servis Filmsetting Ltd, Stockport, Cheshire
Printed and bound in USA by RR Donnelley

The publisher has used its best endeavours to ensure that the URLs for external websites referred to in this book are correct and active at the time of going to press. However, the publisher has no responsibility for the websites and can make no guarantee that a site will remain live or that the content is or will remain appropriate.

Every effort has been made to trace all copyright holders, but if any have been inadvertently overlooked the publisher will be pleased to include any necessary credits in any subsequent reprint or edition.

For further information on Polity, visit our website: politybooks.com

For Frank Dobbin and Michèle Lamont

Contents

Tables and Sidebars

Tables

Sidebars

Preface

The last several years have seen a worldwide outpouring of protest, by citizens in North Africa and the Middle East, Tea Partiers and Wisconsin public employees in the US, the Indignados in Spain, Occupiers around the world, anti-austerity rioters in Europe, Iran's green movement, Istanbul's Taksim Square, Kiev's revolutionaries, and many others. But we should not forget, as we congratulate ourselves for living through an important moment in world history, that protest occurs every day, around the planet, and it always has. Most of the time we don't even hear about it – it is not dramatic or sustained long enough for the media to cover it. Protest is a fundamental part of human existence, and every period in history has the potential to bring about important changes.

Social movements are the form that protest takes most often in today's world. They give regular people an opportunity to explore, articulate, and live out their most basic moral intuitions and principles. Individuals join together to try to recruit, persuade, and inspire others, using all the tools they can find: money, media, stories, collective identities, jokes, cartoons, and sometimes weapons. Some participate casually and sporadically, while others devote their lives to a series of deeply felt causes.

In a cynical world, where we suspect self-interest behind the most seemingly altruistic actions, it might appear hard to understand people who give up material comforts, financial stability, time with family, a normal life, in favor of moral projects and risky tactics that seem to have a vanishingly small chance of

ix

success. Who are these people, who often provide such benefits for our society, while taking relatively few for themselves? What motivates them? How do they think about the world? What helps them win or makes them lose?

In recent years scholars who study social movements have come more and more to appreciate the cultural meanings and feelings that accompany protest, and the ways that people weave these together to make sense of their lives and advance their moral dreams. Protestors and those they engage "feel their way" through actions and decisions, expressing and creating their own goals and identities as well as sifting through a variety of tactics to try to get what they want. We can't understand social movements without understanding participants' points of view.

Looking at voluntary collective action for a cause is also a good way to see how culture works, because central to any social movement is the effort to create new meanings. Nowhere is the creation of culture, or its effects on the world we live in, more obvious. We need to appreciate culture to understand protest, but protest also helps us to understand where culture comes from.

Culture is meaning: how we make sense of the world, including how we understand our own actions and motives, how we signal them to others, how we understand the actions of others, and figure out who we are and who we wish to be. It is both in our heads and embodied in physical carriers such as a couple of words painted on a sheet to make a banner to carry in a march. It is both a continuous process and the occasional products of that process.

One aspect of culture consists of the many emotions that give cognitive understandings their power to attract attention or motivate action. Feelings are present in every stage and every aspect of protest, just as they are there in all human life. Once thought to be a source of irrationality, emotions can also aid us in making decisions and pursuing our goals. Indignation, an emotion that combines anger with moral outrage, is the heart of protest, the first signal that we feel there is something wrong in the world that must be fixed. It also gives us the energy to try to fix it.

Strategy is another cultural dimension of protest: decisions about goals and the means to pursue them; the creation of alliances and the identification of opponents; the mobilization of resources to enable the tactics we select. Strategic choices are rarely straightforward; there are innumerable puzzles and dilemmas that protestors must negotiate. For every choice, there are costs and dangers alongside the promises and benefits. As we proceed, I will identify some of the most common of these tradeoffs, because to understand how protestors do what they do (and whether they win or lose), we need to watch them struggle with these dilemmas. (Tradeoffs become dilemmas when decision-makers recognize and grapple with them.) We can't understand how they make strategic decisions except through the cultural meanings that they have available or which they invent. Even the most pedestrian choices are filtered through a cultural lens.

I will use three labels, *social movement, protest movement,* and *protest,* almost interchangeably. Most social movements are protest movements, focused on what participants find offensive in their world, even though they may also go on to develop positive proposals for alternatives. (Some do and some do not develop ways of doing things differently.) British citizens battling to stop new roads are a protest movement; those promoting craft ales over mass-produced lagers are a social movement. So protest movements are a subset of social movements.

But not all protest takes the form of protest movements: those with complaints may follow normal channels exclusively, satisfied with writing to their elected representatives or to their local newspaper; at the other extreme, some protestors form revolutionary armies instead of protest movements. Often, political parties channel protest without the need for distinct movements; the parties *are* the movement.

Individuals do not always wait for social movements in order to protest. Some find ways to protest all by themselves, in dramatic acts that others cannot ignore, such as hunger strikes or self-immolation. In 1953 India created a new Telugu-speaking state, Andhra Pradesh, in part because one man, named Potti Sreeramulu, starved himself to death to bring attention to this cause. (As I write, other Indians are setting themselves on fire in the hope of splitting a part of Andhra Pradesh off to form yet another new state, just as dozens of Tibetans have done the same to protest China's occupation of their nation.) But if individuals are going to coordinate their protest, they form movements.

At any moment thousands of social movements are active around the world. Even those readers who participate in one or two social movements will encounter most other movements by reading about them and seeing them on television. What should we ask about them when we read about them? How do we get beneath the biases of media coverage? How can we make sense of what they are up to? We need to approach them with a cultural lens.

I have taught graduate and undergraduate courses on social movements since 1987, and I have learned more from my students than they have from me. Many or most had been activists before taking my class, while taking it, or after taking it. The causes have changed, from AIDS and gay and lesbian rights in the early years to global justice and the Occupy movements more recently, but similar challenges and dilemmas have confronted them all. My students at the CUNY Graduate Center – itself a protected space that nurtures political activism – have been especially helpful as I have tried to figure out what happens during political engagement. I thank them all, and especially Kevin Moran, Marisa Tramontano, and Gabriele Cappelletti for their research assistance. The weekly Politics and Protest Workshop at the Grad Center gave me extensive comments, and Liz Borland and her students at the College of New Jersey generously did a test run of the manuscript and provided excellent feedback. Naomi Gerstel, A. K. Thompson, and Jonathan Smucker provided far-reaching commentaries on earlier drafts. I also thank the Netherlands Institute for Advanced Study in the Humanities and Social Sciences in Wassenaar, which provided food, lodging, fellowship, and a charming office where I wrote the first draft of *Protest*.

I try in this book to give an introduction to protest and social movements that highlights action and intention – the subjective – without ignoring structure and constraints. It covers the main kinds of questions that researchers have asked about social movements and related engagements in recent decades, presenting these in a style that I hope any reader can understand. To make the book classroom-friendly, I have placed in jarring **boldface** the concepts that I think a student should know after reading the book, using italics for lists and other normal kinds of writing emphasis. (Thus **bloc recruitment** is in bold, while *music* is italicized as part of a list of physical carriers of meaning. I don't think you need me to define music for you.) I have placed the most common dilemmas in sidebars. To make the book more readable I have been sparing in my use of citations, and apologize to all those scholars whose work I could have cited but did not.

Each chapter begins with a case that I then exploit for evidence to illustrate my themes in the remainder of the chapter. I have tried to mix important historical movements like "Wilkes and Liberty" and the women's movement with recent efforts like Occupy, as well as including one rightwing movement, the US Christian Right, and one attempted revolution, in Egypt. For those who would like to read more, including graduate students preparing to take examinations in the field of social movements, I have placed asterisks next to some of the entries in the bibliography because I think they would add up to a good survey of the field. I welcome feedback via email: jjasper@gc.cuny.edu.

Introduction: Doing Protest

Joyous bivouacs: Occupy Wall Street

For two exciting months in the fall of 2011, Occupy Wall Street held the world's attention and inspired similar camps elsewhere. The initial occupation on September 17 was organized by an email blast from Adbusters, an anti-consumerist group known for its "subvertisements" – humorous spoofs of popular commercials.

Almost immediately, the militants occupying Zuccotti Park adopted the label "99 percent" and its companion "1 percent," which summarized most Americans' moral disgust with neoliberal policies pursued by both Republicans and Democrats since 1981. It was a brilliant pair of terms that implied solidarity with the vast majority and defined a villain that had arrogantly usurped more than its share of the economic pie. This was exactly the kind of **moral battery** – a pair of contrasting emotions, one positive and the other negative – that generates indignation and attracts people toward the good pole.

The movement's other great term was "occupy" itself, a tactical invitation that was soon applied to hundreds of figurative as well as physical places: Occupy Oakland, Occupy Toledo, Occupy Patriarchy, Occupy the SEC, Occupy Our Homes, Occupy Shabbat, Occupy Boehner, Occupy da Hood, or Cyprus's Occupy Buffer Zone.

The Occupiers used general assemblies, GA, to make decisions.

1

Lengthy meetings at which all speakers were welcomed, they were supposed to arrive at a consensus. The "people's mic," by which the audience repeated each of a speaker's phrases, forced the entire group to articulate each thought as well as conveying it to those at the back of the crowd. Several simple hand gestures gave automatic feedback and made the lengthy meetings more fun and engaging. Protestors camping at Zuccotti Park had plenty of time to devote to participatory democracy, a cumbersome process nonetheless thrilling to those for whom "real" democracy is a core moral aspiration. Here was a new way of living that was far more democratic than anything they had experienced before. Democracy in the GA was either tempered or enhanced by "progressive stacks," which moved certain people – considered underrepresented or disadvantaged or who had not yet spoken – ahead in the queue.

Mainstream news media, looking for an easy hook, complained that the movement had no demands, no policies it wanted President Obama or Governor Cuomo to enact. Indeed, it would not have been easy to extract precise proposals, much less elaborate plans, from the sprawling GA. But that was not the point, as one beaming fellow expressed with his poster's adaptation of a queer slogan: "We're here, we're unclear, get used to it." The Occupiers were clear enough about their indignation at economic inequality, united – like many movements – by their feelings more than by glib slogans or explicit policy proposals. Precise demands would have granted politicians too much legitimacy and power, making the Occupiers into powerless plaintiffs before the authorities.

Occupy Wall Street faced the same strategic dilemmas that most protests do. One was the **Janus dilemma**: how much time do you devote to internal issues and processes, like the GA or providing food to campers, building the sense of community that provided the biggest thrill of life at Zuccotti, versus how much time do you devote to other players outside the movement, such as the media, the police, or allies like unions? Occupy always risked turning inward, becoming a festival of internal democracy, a joyous bivouac, satisfying in and of itself. But the regular marches and events elsewhere in New York balanced this, making Occupy a

The Janus dilemma

Janus was the Roman god in charge of gates and doorways, who often appeared above the door on each side, with one face looking outward and the other inward. Some activities and arguments are aimed at a movement's own members, while others are aimed at outside players such as opponents, the state, and bystanders. Every movement does both, and must find the right balance. A movement can become overly inward, having meetings to motivate its members, reinforce their collective solidarity, and help them enjoy themselves. At the other extreme it can focus exclusively on external interactions, letting its members follow along or not. Eventually they stop following. Various decisions fall under the Janus dilemma: do you encourage a collective identity that emphasizes similarity to the broader society, or one that highlights difference (Bernstein 1997)? Do you pay to hire professional staff, or do you rely on volunteers from within, motivated by their enthusiasm and solidarity (Mansbridge 1986)? Do you spend more time on participatory meetings, or on carrying out the decisions they make (although internal democracy also has external benefits such as good public relations, and hopefully good strategic choices too.)?

player on a world media stage. Almost all social movements must grapple with the Janus dilemma, which in this case often echoed tensions between full-time and part-time participants.

Just as important were two dilemmas about internal organization. The **organization dilemma** is about how many rules to have governing your procedures: rules make things predictable, but in doing so they constrict what you can do. The **pyramid dilemma** is about how much vertical hierarchy to build into your group or organization: it can be efficient or pleasurable to have strong leaders, but they sometimes substitute their own goals for those of the rest of the participants. These dilemmas interacted in the case of Occupy: the formal rules about how to make decisions and how to run the GA were meant to keep the pyramid low, horizontal

Different generations of activists mix at Zuccotti Park. Credit: JMJ.

instead of vertical (although this did not prevent informal leaders from emerging).

Many Occupiers insisted they had little in common with the global justice movement that had been born in Seattle in 1999 (see chapter 6). Part of this distancing was generational, since successive cohorts of new protestors have different sensibilities from those who joined only a year or two earlier. Part was a genuine concern for nonviolence, arising out of a sense that the masked "black bloc" of anarchists who had broken windows in Seattle had tarnished the movement's reputation (the naughty or nice dilemma, as we'll see later).

Occupy had a big impact on those who were part of it, giving them a glimpse of a more exciting, participatory world, but also giving them a crash course in political tactics (Gitlin 2012). They will take the hopes and the know-how with them to future campaigns, in protest movements yet to be imagined. But Occupy also wanted to have an external impact. Extreme inequality has not diminished, and no new policies were enacted to deal with it, except possibly Cuomo's decision to support a tax on New York's millionaires.

Yet the encampments received extensive media coverage, and more favorable coverage than most protest gets. The media treated the Occupiers as real people with serious grievances, for the most part, even if they often portrayed them as grubby, unemployed young people – an earnest kind of slacker – with unrealistic utopian dreams. Beyond the direct coverage of the protests, articles and editorials began to appear about inequality in the United States, accepting it as a public problem that policymakers needed to take seriously. Coverage of the Tea Party, the rightwing group that one year earlier had tapped into some of the same populist anger as Occupy, shrank, with less impact on the 2012 elections than in 2010. Occupy's effect may have been indirect, but it was not negligible.

Social movements

In common usage **social movements** are sustained, intentional efforts to foster or retard broad legal and social changes, primarily outside the normal institutional channels endorsed by authorities. "Sustained" implies that movements differ from single events such as rallies, which are the primary activities sponsored by most movements. Movements' persistence often allows them to develop formal organizations, but they also operate through informal social networks.

The word "intentional" links movements to culture and strategy: people have ideas about what they want and how to get it, ideas that are filtered through culture as well as individual psychology. Movements have purposes, even when these have to do with transforming members themselves (as in many religious or self-help movements) rather than the world outside the movement.

"Foster or retard": although many scholars define movements as progressive, dismissing regressive efforts as **countermovements,** this distinction seems arbitrary (not to mention the unfortunate effect that different tools are then used to analyze the two types).

The anti-abortion movement is just as much a social movement as the abortion-rights movement, even if it wishes to turn back the clock on human rights, at least according to feminists.

"Non-institutional" distinguishes movements from political parties and interest groups that are a regular, stably funded part of most political systems, even though movements frequently create these other entities and often maintain close relationships with existing ones. Some protest groups evolve into interest groups or political parties.

Despite this definition, there is no clear boundary between social movements and other phenomena such as revolutions, riots, political parties, and interest groups. The more of each component – persistence, intention, a concern with change, and outside normal institutions – that we see, the more we want to call something a social movement. The less we see, the more we search for other labels. Rioters may share some of the goals of a protest movement without acting explicitly on behalf of that movement (yet most rioters choose their targets carefully, expressing their feelings of indignation and sense of blame, and so implicitly share a movement's goals). They may show their political anger and frustration – yet at the same time grab a bottle of perfume from a broken storefront. Humans always have multiple motivations, which is why we need a cultural perspective to make their actions intelligible.

Throughout this book I use the words "activist" and "protestor" for people who are doing protest. But a word of caution: this does that mean that some people are born protestors, with unusual personalities that distinguish them from other people, any more than "students" or "professors" are defined by this one activity. Protestors are not some inherently distinct subspecies of human; any of us might end up in a social movement.

Just as multiple activities are involved, so there is no single question to answer about social movements, but a series of questions. Why does protest appear when it does? Who first imagines a movement, or expresses its vision? Who joins the movement? Who continues and who drops out along the way? What do protestors do? How do they decide what to do? When do they change their tactics? When do they win, when do they lose? What other effects do they have? When do movements end? No single theory, and certainly no simple theory, can answer all these questions. We need different ways to explain each of them, although each explanation will contain a cultural dimension.

Culture

Culture is composed of shared thoughts, feelings, and morals, along with the physical embodiments we create to express or shape them. It is through cultural processes – from singing to reading to marching together down a street – that we give the world meaning, that we understand ourselves and others. Culture permeates protestors' actions, and also those of all the other players with whom they interact, such as judges, police, legislators, reporters, and others. We need to understand both sides – or many sides – in a conflict.

Culture has three main components. For one thing, it consists of **cognition**: the words we use, the beliefs we have about the world, the claims we make about how the world is, the distinctions we draw between one thing and another (between one group and another, for instance). These include frames, such as "the 99 percent," implying a theory of victims, a theory of villains (the 1 percent), and a diagnosis of the problem, namely the enormous gap between the two. They also include collective identities, in this case again the 99 percent and the 1 percent. Stories, each with a beginning, a middle, and an end, are also part of cognition. Even tactics, such as "occupy," are ways to tap into culturally formed understandings of how to act.

Scholars like to analyze these cognitive elements of culture because they are easy to detach from action, to list in a table, to identify by reading brochures and transcripts of speeches. But in taking them out of context like this, we risk losing sight of how people experience these ideas, how they use them to persuade others, how they are motivated by them. People don't carry their ideas in their heads like books on a library shelf; they live them out through their actions.

Emotions, the second part of culture, keep us closer to people's actual lives, because humans feel their way through situations more than they consciously think about them. Emotions have a bad reputation, since the philosophers who tend to write about them prefer to talk about abstract thoughts instead of the messy act of thinking, ideas over feelings, products over processes. They have portrayed emotions as the opposite of thinking, as unfortunate interferences that lead us to do dumb things. Only recently have psychologists shown that emotions also send us signals and help us process information, evaluate our situations, and begin to formulate paths of action. Far from always disrupting our lives, emotions help us carry on. They are functional, sometimes even wise. They are a part of sensible actions as well as regrettable ones. They are neither good nor bad, but simply normal. Emotions are part of culture because we learn when and how to display them, and what to call them (fear versus anger, for instance). They also permeate cognition: emotions bring stories to life, make us care about collective identities, help us hate villains or pity victims. Cognition and emotion are inseparable.

In addition to cognition and emotions, **morality** is the third component of culture. It consists of two parts. One is a set of explicit *principles*, like "Do unto others as you would have them do unto you," or "From each according to his ability, to each according to his need." We formulate statements like these in order to persuade others or to indoctrinate children in our viewpoint. It is the second part of morality that actually drives actions most of the time, in the form of *intuitions* that are felt rather than explicitly formulated. When we blush over an indiscretion or wince when we see a horse whipped, we may not be able to say exactly why. But our feelings are telling us that we know something is wrong. More people are led into politics by their moral intuitions than by their principles. The principles usually come later. Our emotions help us think, including thinking about right and wrong.

Cognition, emotion, and morality are usually all present in real-life political statements and actions, constantly shaping each other. We distinguish them only when we analyze those concrete cases.

Culture is not just in our heads (and hearts). A photo captures a protest group's indignation, analysis, and anger. A book may elaborate a movement's ideology or philosophy, for instance demonstrating in detail, complete with photos, the impact of inequality on the poor and the urgency of fixing the problem. Actions also express meanings. A march is carefully choreographed to send a message about who the demonstrators are, what they want, or who is blocking them. Rituals eventually develop to express a group's fundamental beliefs and feelings, reminding insiders as well as outsiders about who they are.

These physical embodiments of meanings don't matter much if they don't correspond to our internal feelings, but they often help us to sustain those meanings, focus on certain ones rather than others, and transmit them to new people. Once embodied, meanings can travel: an Occupier carried a poster saying, "I'll believe corporations are people when Texas executes one," a lovely dig at the death penalty as well as the myth of corporations as individuals with inalienable rights. She was photographed, then her image made it into websites, newspapers, and eventually books, with her crisp message available to new audiences at each step.

Not culture

Culture is everywhere, but it is not everything. If there were nothing except culture, that would actually make it less useful as a concept. It would fail what I call the "oxygen test" in social science: there would be no social life without oxygen, but adding it to our explanatory models isn't very useful. We can assume its existence, and move on.

So what is not culture? **Resources**, for one thing: money and the physical things it can buy. These include guns that shoot bullets, a bullhorn that makes our voices travel further, antennas that transmit radio broadcasts. **Arenas** are also not culture, but the places where strategic action occurs, governed by formal rules and informal traditions, and in which resources are only used in certain ways. (Scholars often refer to these as **political structures**.)

Finally, **individuals** have a number of idiosyncratic ways that they think and feel about the world which, because no one else shares them, are not culture. This is **psychology**. They may be psychotic hallucinations, or they may instead be creative ideas that have simply *not yet* been shared with others (if they never get shared, they are not culture). When we see two people at the same rally, we assume they share goals and understandings of the event, but their agreement is rarely perfect, and they sometimes disagree enormously. Occupiers refused to state explicit demands because they recognized that people could be drawn to the encampments for a lot of reasons, and they did not want to exclude anyone (they even welcomed some members of the 1 percent).

Even though resources, arenas, and psychology are not culture, they interact closely with it, and this is one of the strengths of a cultural perspective. Culture helps us understand the other dimensions. A bullhorn has little impact sitting on a shelf in an activist's mother's closet; it matters when it amplifies words to an eager audience. On the opposite side of the battle, cans of pepper spray or tear gas do nothing by themselves. Police commanders must issue commands to use them; their forces must decide whether to obey. These choices reflect the calculations, sympathies, fears, and moral intuitions of the "forces of order," in other words culture. (An individual officer may be sadistic or angry and use pepper spray even when ordered not to, a psychological more than a cultural factor, but he may then be disciplined as a result – depending on the culture of the larger police force, media attention, pressure from politicians, and so on.)

Occasionally, resources have an impact without being used: when their very existence is a reminder or a threat that they *could* be used if necessary. Again, this requires cultural interpretation on both sides, by those threatening and those being threatened. They constantly try to understand each other. Protestors ask themselves if they should take those threats seriously.

Nor do structured arenas do much without culture. First, they reflect the cultural understandings and strategic goals of those who established them, intending to constrain future interactions in desired ways. Arenas provide rules to which strategic players can refer, they suggest certain ways of understanding goals and actions, and they structure the costs and hazards, advantages and promise of actions. They must still be interpreted. Their rules and traditions are there for strategic players to refer to, rely upon, and subvert.

Even more structurally, arenas contain buildings, rooms, and decorations that channel the cultural interpretation and the actions that occur there. Zuccotti Park offered places to sleep, sit, debate, and drum (but not to defecate), all with some protection from the outside, although not so much as to isolate protestors from tourists (or neighbors from the sound of drumming). It had to be converted into an arena, its physical resources recognized as useful for an encampment.

Structures such as arenas consist of cultural blueprints or schemas linked to physical resources and places. Laws and other rules are the most obvious schemas, usually elaborated over time through explicit debate and enforced by a state with a police force and army. But we also develop informal expectations about what people are supposed to do in an arena, what is proper and improper behavior there. The rules of arenas shape action, but a lot of protest is also aimed at changing those very rules. Although Occupy was unable to change the rules of how incomes are distributed in capitalist America, it forced some police – reluctantly – into better behavior, and it pushed some trade-union members to more militant tactics.

Culture also shapes many of the idiosyncratic understandings that individuals can hold. Even the unfortunate psychoses of the mentally ill echo their experiences and interpretations of their broader culture. The innovations and distinctive perspectives of all individuals reflect all their past experiences, as they accumulate unique collections of cultural understandings from a lifelong series of situations and interactions. Our minds act like filters, capturing bits of memorable information and felt associations. This is the reason that individuals can be creative, seeing a situation in a unique way, recalling and applying what they learned from related situations in the past. It took some clever individuals to see Zuccotti Park as a place to plant and grow a social movement, although they came to this after marching to another site only to find that its owners, alerted by listserv discussions, had fenced it off. (Zuccotti's owners could not do this because of New York City laws governing "privately owned public spaces.") Psychology and culture, but also resources, help people adapt quickly.

In the rest of the book I will talk about ways that resources, arenas, individuals, and culture interact with each other, but we should not exaggerate the distinction. Any action has elements of all these: individual humans use physical resources and their own bodies to express cultural meanings to each other and outside audiences, in particular arenas. The distinction is what philosophers call *analytic*: resources and the rest are dimensions of action that we can highlight or hide so that we can understand how people pull off their projects, how they do what they do. Like resources and arenas, culture does nothing by itself. Only people do things. But they do things *with* objects, just as the video clips and live streaming of protests allowed Occupiers to challenge police accounts and gain sympathy from millions of viewers. We might say that people and objects collaborate with each other.

Looking ahead

We run a risk in talking so much about protestors and their actions, decisions, and visions: it may seem as though it is easy for them to get their way. The opposite is true: *most protest fails.* Scholars of social movements do not always like to admit this, since they most often study movements they admire. But whether movements win or lose, or do something in between, we need to understand why. Protest groups with lots of resources, brilliant frames and stories, sympathetic identities, extensive media coverage, and clever strategies still often lose. They face constraints that they just cannot overcome. The Occupy movement had many small successes, but it was hardly able to rein in capitalism. One reason is that other players also have their resources, ideologies, and strategies. Against every anti-corporate campaign, the targeted companies deploy their own money, pressure their political allies, take out newspaper ads disguised as editorials, and fight back in every way they can, every day. Arenas have losers as well as winners, and arenas are often set up to advantage one player over others.

This book tries to provide some historical perspective, never a bad thing. The excitement of Zuccotti Park resonates back in time. One commentator, pointing out the similarities in French protests of 1848, 1871, 1936, and 1968, described them as **moments of madness** (Zolberg 2008: 30, 31):

> Liberated from the constraints of time, place, and circumstance, from history, men and women choose their parts from the available repertory or forge new ones in an act of creation. Dreams become possibilities . . . What they failed to achieve in 1936 was at the center of their aspirations 32 years later when the factories were again turned into joyous bivouacs in the name of participation.

The year 2011 was another moment when dreams seemed possible, in joyous bivouacs such as Tahrir Square, Rothschild Boulevard, Puerta del Sol, and Zuccotti Park.

The following chapters come in what I hope is a logical order. We first ask more about what protest and social movements are; then we examine the many ways that humans impose meaning on their worlds; next we look at the ways in which political and economic infrastructures aid protest. In chapters 4 through 6 we ask how movements recruit new members, motivate old ones, and make decisions. Chapter 7 looks at how protestors engage other players, and chapter 8 examines their wins, losses, and other impacts on today's world.

Most chapter titles emphasize action rather than completed acts: recruiting rather than recruitment, deciding rather than decisions. I want to emphasize that people are *doing protest*: it does not just happen thanks to impersonal processes without subjects or because of mysterious creatures called "protestors". People do protest every day, but it happens less often than we might expect, given how much discontent there is in the world. Most of the time people shrug off their complaints or crack a joke to friends. Only occasionally do they organize with others. We can't forget that social movements are special, fleeting, fragile – and often heroic. They can change our world. Protestors are the heroes of the modern age.

1

What are Social Movements?

The street as an arena: the Wilkes movement

John Wilkes was one of the most memorable Englishman of the eighteenth century. Cross-eyed and generally unattractive, he was witty and charming, what used to be called "a lady's man," and one of the most aggressive muckrakers of any era. Separated from a wealthy wife, whose fortune gave him a seat in parliament in 1757 (it cost him £7,000), he was indignant when his faction of the Whig Party was excluded from government in 1762. Wilkes launched a weekly pamphlet, *The North Briton*, for the sole purpose of attacking King George III and his appointed prime minister, the incompetent Lord Bute. One of his innovations was to name the government ministers he was attacking instead of using the customary initials followed by dashes (Lord B——). Within a year Wilkes was indicted for treasonous libel when, in issue number 45, he suggested that King George had lied in a speech to parliament.

Over the next several years Wilkes won a remarkable series of legal victories against the King and government, striking down search warrants against unnamed persons, allowing newspapers to reprint parliamentary debates, and preventing parliament from overturning elections simply because it found a candidate unsuitable. The number "45" became a common graffito, proudly scrawled on doors and walls, and "Wilkes and Liberty" became a rallying cry for a number of related causes. Wilkes, who siphoned considerable money from his charities to buy alcohol and prostitutes, became a symbol of sundry types of liberty. Large mobs formed to support his re-elections to parliament, as the King clumsily intervened against him. According to sociologist Charles Tilly (1995, 2004), these mobs – part election campaign, part agitation for civil liberties, and part drunken festival – comprised the first modern social movement.

There were several components to this new political vehicle. Wilkes was a master of the media, not only writing obscene attacks on Bute and the King (and the King's mother), but also attracting attention for his dramatic actions and pithy quotes (yesteryear's soundbites). In addition, he brought together two arenas that had been separate: parliament and the street. His followers organized marches and rallies to put pressure on elected officials, and much of that pressure was devoted to the rights of association, assembly, and free speech – the central tools of the social movement. They borrowed from guild ceremonies, veterans' parades, Methodist revival meetings, and more. There were more coercive tactics, too, such as stopping carriages and forcing the fancy occupants to shout "Wilkes and Liberty," but the balance of tactics overall was shifting from force to persuasion. The street was increasingly important as a political arena.

Wilkes was a pioneer in another way: although the largest mobs were in London, where they could intimidate politicians and the royal family, they could also be found in towns around Britain, eagerly following the newspapers that had become cheap and ubiquitous. There were new webs of political influence, with which protestors became entangled, learning to interact on the basis of new indignation and claims, with new kinds of players, and with new hopes.

Here we see the importance of remarkable individuals, with personality quirks and idiosyncratic motivations, but they get their way through social movements in familiar ways: by forming social networks, exploiting the news media, and getting people into the streets to pressure officials.

The modern social movement

People protest in whatever ways they can. Slaves, servants, and others under close surveillance find subtle means, such as spitting in the master's food, playing dumb when given orders, performing tasks in a shoddy way, stealing or breaking valuables. If challenged, they can sometimes deny any intention of resistance, although this does not always prevent a beating (Scott 1985). Some of these **weapons of the weak** provide only private satisfaction or gain, but others are performed with audiences in mind. Some require solidarity, such as private jokes, gossip, and rumors that undermine the perceived power and dignity of your oppressors. Something as simple as rolling your eyes can undermine authority, with its suggestion of how silly or clueless the boss is.

Subordinates are usually cautious about their resistance, especially when they can be killed for insubordination. They rely on **hidden transcripts,** meanings that run counter to the dominant viewpoints and are expressed privately, in order to understand and criticize their situations (Scott 1990). This kind of surreptitious resistance can nonetheless leave a public impression, as with graffiti that thousands of passers-by can view. Other weapons of the weak are more coercive than persuasive – barn burning, the maiming of livestock – although a burning building not only does direct damage but also sends a message: it can be seen for miles, broadcasting the existence of resistance and encouraging copycats.

By placing people closer together in greater anonymity, cities encourage different forms of protest, especially riots and other kinds of crowd actions. It takes less advance planning to get a crowd together in a city than in the countryside. Even ancient cities had disruptive crowds. In Alexandria, Egypt in 485CE, when a new student was hazed – in truth, beaten up – by older ones, the local Christian community interpreted the event as an anti-Christian attack and within 48 hours the bishop had rounded up enough of his flock to sack a nearby pagan temple. In the following weeks, the pagans fought back through an official investigation, but the political trajectory toward Christian dominance was clear. Also clear was the bishop's manipulation of rumors to fabricate an opportunity to attack his rivals (Watts 2010). Christianity – one of the world's most successful religious movements – did not conquer the Roman Empire by turning the other cheek.

Although humans have always found ways to show their displeasure, the social movement, as we recognize it today, arose in the modern world. We might even say that it emerged in late eighteenth-century Britain and America, partly to take advantage of increasingly powerful parliaments grounded on the idea of citizenship (even if parliament is known as Congress in the US). These new arenas contributed even more than urbanization to the birth of the social movement. As in other countries, later, social movements demanded rights and recognition for groups that were excluded from political participation but that felt they were part of the nation. The very idea of the "nation" implies a "people" with some solidarity just by virtue of where they were born or the blood in their veins, regardless of their social class. If we are all "English" or "Russian," how can some own others as serfs, or rule us without our consent? Ideas about freedom and democracy spread widely in the eighteenth century, even though few governments acted on them – yet.

Democracy is both a goal and a means for movements. It promises a great deal (promises that even today are not entirely fulfilled anywhere). It offers *protections* from arbitrary actions by the state (human rights), as well as several political rights: some *participation* in government decisions, or at least major decisions; some *accountability* by the state for its actions, and especially its mistakes; and some *transparency* in how it makes decisions and takes action. In addition to these elements of political citizenship, later forms of democracy have also promised some minimal level of economic *well-being*: health, housing, food. When groups feel that their government is failing to provide such things, they learn to band together into social movements. Because regimes that claim to be democratic promise so many things, ironically, there are more potential sources of indignation than in autocratic regimes. Expectations are higher.

Some sort of elected legislature is the centerpiece of democracy, and social movements arose to pressure the representatives in those bodies. In 50 years of research on France and Britain, Tilly (1986, 1995) showed how protest gradually shifted in the eighteenth and nineteenth centuries from *direct* attacks on landlords, tax collectors, misbehaving neighbors, and other targets of indignation, to *indirect* efforts – through letters, petitions, and public demonstrations – to sway elected officials. Participants less often pulled and burned down houses, tarred and feathered their targets, or played raucous music beneath the window of someone who had broken village norms. More often they made speeches, marched through the streets chanting slogans and singing songs, and painted banners and signs. They now sent messages to elected officials, the media, and the broader public.

A legislature is one example of a strategic arena. Courtrooms are another, an especially well-defined arena with clear rules about who can participate and what they can do. News media are another arena, less clearly defined, in which players struggle over what statements and images will appear on websites, television broadcasts, and printed newspapers. Protestors usually promote their causes in several arenas at the same time. Blocked in one, they may try to enter another, seeking an arena where their resources and personnel have the most advantage (much like seeking the high ground on a field of battle). A modern society offers dozens of arenas to potential protestors.

Arenas offer openings for some kinds of protest and discourage other kinds. For this reason they have been called **political opportunity structures**, since they sometimes provide opportunities for protestors to mobilize large numbers of supporters and to win concessions from the state. An entire theory of protest was built on this idea, as we'll see. Because researchers in this tradition focused on the state, they showed that different nations have different political opportunity structures and, as a result, different kinds of protest (Kriesi et al. 1995). In some countries political parties are more open to new demands, providing an opportunity for protestors, while in other nations parties adhere to ideologies that preclude openings to new issues. In Germany and the United States, legal courts have a lot of authority, so protestors file lawsuits; they do not file many suits in France, where courts have less power. Protestors use the channels available to them. They may also try to invent new arenas or modify existing ones, like the Wilkites who pursued new legal rights.

In addition to these long-run **structural horizons**, political opportunities also come in short-run versions, **windows of opportunity** that open or close. When a gunman kills 20 children in a school, citizens send letters and march in the streets to demand stricter controls on firearms; politicians see a chance to win votes by supporting these controls; and the news media draw in audiences by reporting on all of it. Oil spills, nuclear accidents, and other disasters can also focus attention for a while, with just enough time to mobilize some protest. After a few weeks or a few months, attention turns elsewhere, and the window of opportunity closes. Wilkes's supporters seized the opportunity offered by the government whenever it harassed, jailed, or barred Wilkes from taking the parliamentary seat to which he had been elected. Every new outrage was a short window for mobilizing the street. Even today, outrageous government actions are probably the most common windows of opportunity.

We can see how "Wilkes and Liberty" helped define social movements by comparing it to our definition. It was sustained, or at least it reappeared with great regularity as long as Wilkes was battling Bute and the King. Its intentions were clear enough, encompassing both specific protections for Wilkes and broader rights for all. It was outside the normal political channels that authorities controlled. But the agitation fell short in a couple ways. It relied on and reinforced social networks that could be reused, but it did not generate formal organizations other than Wilkes's original newspaper. And it only gradually came to formulate its demands in broad ideological terms, putting aside the specific demands on Wilkes's behalf. Wilkes and his supporters were feeling their way to a new form of protest. (Before Wilkes, protest had fallen short of full social movement status in even more ways.)

In the United States the social movement developed in two stages. The Revolution relied on the networks, rallies, and rhetoric of the protest movement that had formed in response to a series of unpopular actions by the British government, most notably the 1765

Stamp Act (which imposed a tax, payable only in British currency, on the kind of paper used for newspapers and printed documents – precisely the media colonists were using to express their opinions and make their demands). The colonists considered themselves British citizens but they had no representatives in parliament: just the kind of situation that raises expectations – and frustrations.

The next step occurred in the 1830s, as a wave of national movements linked personal choices to public problems, the most prominent "sins" being slavery and alcohol. From now on moral reformers would hold individuals personally responsible for far-flung evils. They built national networks, often beginning with Baptist and Methodist preachers, developed a massive publishing and mailing industry, boycotted certain merchants, used direct, illegal actions to tackle the "sins," and formed their own parties and lobbying organizations (with bylaws, regular meetings, and elected leaders) – tactics still deployed by today's protest movements (Young 2006).

The social movement of today attempts to send messages to a variety of audiences, especially its own members and potential members, but also legislators, other agencies of the state, and the media. Movements formulate moral visions and try to entice others to share in them. But even if they specialize in persuasion and performance, they have not entirely given up other means of getting their way.

Coercion, money, words

These are the three great families of means that people employ in their strategic engagements, whether those are business deals or wars, politics or protest. They try to get their way through physical force or blockage, by paying people, or by persuading them. Social movements, even though they may use all three, are largely defined by their specialization in persuasion. To the extent they rely on coercion instead, they shade into revolutionary armies or criminal gangs; to the extent they rely on money instead they become bureaucratic interest groups.

Because of the importance of persuasion, it is especially useful to understand social movements through the lens of **rhetoric**, namely culture deployed in order to have an effect on others, with public speeches as the original model. A related perspective is to see politics as a set of performances embodying information, feelings, and morals intended to inspire others (Alexander 2011). In either case we view strategic players as audiences for each other's words and actions (although money and coercion also have cultural components: they must be interpreted). Like an orator in a public square, movements seek audiences and try to persuade them to feel, believe, or act in a certain way. And even in the age of the internet, much communication still takes place via orators in public squares, from Zuccotti to Tahrir.

In non-democratic regimes – which include the majority of states that have existed in human history – public issues are mostly settled by physical force. Nations go to war over disputed territories; a monarch suppresses revolt by chopping off hundreds of heads. In some settings even today, violence (or the threat of violence) prevails – especially police violence directed against protestors. Rhetoric arose in the ancient Greek world at the same time democracy did, as an alternative to coercion; now you might hope to persuade others, especially to vote a certain way in the assembly or on juries.

Social movements may be linked to democracy and to persuasion, but they also sometimes resort to physical force, as when striking workers obstruct an assembly line or rioters ransack a shop. As we'll see in chapter 7, coercion is a risky strategy for protestors, often succeeding by embarrassing the authorities, but even more often failing because it allows authorities to justify severe repression. Some militants are pushed to violent, even military, means in response to actions by the state.

This is where revolutions come from: there is no other way to change a despised regime than by overthrowing it (as Jeff Goodwin suggests in the title of his book about revolutions, *No Other Way Out*). When regimes systematically prevent public participation, and tiny elites monopolize the military, media, and economy, revolution becomes a common goal for protestors.

Unions and leftwing parties often make seizure of the state their primary goal, but most social movements today want to influence the state, not own it.

Coercion comes in violent and nonviolent forms. It is one thing to break the law by stopping traffic, another to break store windows, and a very different action to break people's bones. Almost all social movements today advocate the civil disobedience of occupations and blockages; almost all condemn violence against humans. In between, their attitudes toward the kinds of riots that damage property, whether sabotage of machines or smashing store windows, has varied a lot across movements and over time.

On top of age-old methods of coercion and the forms of persuasion that arose with democracy, the modern world (roughly the last 500 years) has seen the rapid spread of a third way to get people to do what you want them to: pay them. You can almost always find people who will do the work merely for the money. You don't need them to fear you, and they need not agree entirely with your goals (although if they do agree with you, you may not need to pay them as much). The ability to simply hire people is one of the great advantages that states and corporations have over protestors: they do not need to persuade their employees that they are morally right. Although markets have their own drawbacks, they seem preferable to coercion, if not as desirable as persuasion.

Most protest groups use money in one way or another. If nothing else, they buy copy machines and internet services (or someone else has bought and donated them). Groups that flourish are tempted to hire professional staff, rent offices, buy advertising, and adopt other expensive strategies. In order to do this, they usually have to start raising funds. It is a spiral: the more they raise, the more they can spend, and the more they spend, the more they have to raise. Whether that circle is vicious or virtuous, a bad thing or a good one, is much debated by both activists and scholars. Like so many issues that we will examine in this book, it poses a strategic dilemma to activists. Once they start applying for foundation grants or selling social services to government agencies, they become a different kind of group.

The dirty hands dilemma

In a perfect world, means and ends would always fit each other, so that we would always be able to use means that feel morally comfortable to us. But sometimes there are good goals that we just can't achieve with the means we prefer. We may need to use deception, or spies, for instance. For some groups, any use of money is suspect, and they would prefer to operate on a purely volunteer basis. But there are things that only money will buy. Purists are willing to give up on some ends, while pragmatists are willing to dirty their hands a little bit. The difference depends on how strongly we feel morally about the tactic. The flip side of the dirty-hands dilemma concerns favored tactics, which we may become attached to and use even if they are inefficient or incapable of getting us our goals. To exasperated critics, an excess of participatory democracy runs this risk.

Even though the term "interest group" is applied to formal organizations that lobby (instead of protesting) and have staffs, the usual difference between a group and an organization is something else. As I will use it, a **group** is an informal gathering or network, usually small, while an **organization** has bylaws, regular times and places to meet, acknowledged leaders who have the authority to call meetings and make other demands on members, and usually some legal status.

Money will buy physical resources like office space, but it can also buy people's time. An organization can hire a receptionist, a lawyer, a public-relations firm. Once you hire experts, they are especially likely to transform your protest group, advising you to adopt the tactics in which they specialize. The **sorcerer's-apprentice dilemma** is a twist on the dirty-hands dilemma: what was created or hired to be merely a means gets out of control and becomes an end in itself, taking the organization in new, unexpected directions. These may be good directions, but they are just as often unwelcome. Once you hire lawyers, you will adopt legal strategies.

Non-cultural approaches

Today most theories of social movements acknowledge their cultural dimensions, but that has not always been so. Some theories have seen people as driven by a small number of impulses or incentives rather than a broad spectrum of culturally defined goals. And some theories understand social movements by placing them in big historical and structural contexts (the "macrosocial" perspective) rather than starting with actual participants and their points of view (the "microsocial" perspective). Table 1 categorizes traditions according to these two choices that theorists make. We can trace the history of theories by starting in the lower left box with psychological theories, then circling clockwise through successive theories until we get to cultural theories in the lower right.

Grievance theories dominated the study of social movements until the 1970s. They envision a fairly direct line of causation between individuals' internal psychological states and collective political efforts. If enough people are angry and disappointed, they will somehow form protest groups or pour into the streets to riot. They may be disappointed with their own economic situation, for instance if they are hungry, or they may be disappointed with themselves: they may feel uprooted and alienated, they may be searching for meaning or an identity (Klapp 1969).

Table I Four major theoretical orientations

Level of focus	Images of human motivation	
	Restricted incentives	Diverse cultural meanings
Macrosocial	Structural and structural-historical theories: Resource mobilization, political process, Marxism, Tilly	Cultural-historical theories: Touraine
Microsocial	Psychological theories: Crowd theory, grievance theory, Freud, rational choice theory	Cultural theories: Framing, narrative and emotion theories; social psychology

One psychological theory popular in the nineteenth and early twentieth centuries was known as **crowd theory**, which held that if a large enough group of people come together into a crowd (often termed a "mob"), they will do things that they would not normally do as individuals. They will be more emotional and commit violent acts by shedding inhibitions and egging each other on. Theorists in this tradition were elites who did not like protestors very much, and did not think that any good came from this kind of activity.

In Freudian versions of psychological theories, people engage in politics in an effort to mend tensions in their own personalities. One theory from the 1960s posited that protestors are trying to resolve oedipal complexes by attaching all good feelings to the "mother" movement, while associating everything bad with the "father" figures of the state and other dominant institutions (including professors). In addressing internal conflicts, the stick figures in these models are unable to craft reasonable responses to what happens in the world around them, but are stuck repeating the same defenses that they learned in early childhood.

Another psychological theory is known as **rational choice theory**, which features individuals as making decisions in order to maximize a small number of satisfactions, especially having to do with money. Derived from economics, rationalist theories challenged other psychological theories in the mid-1960s (Olson 1965), and have developed elaborate mathematical formulas to describe decision-making. But the elegance of mathematics has led them away from the messy reality of human life. Their equations work best when there is only one quantity to maximize, and especially one that can be quantified. That is why money works so well. Mathematical theories are less adept at understanding how people balance different goals, such as increasing your organization's budget, saving the lives of whales, and thrilling your membership with a big rally. It is hard to compare these. Precise formulas are of limited use in a world of unavoidable tradeoffs and dilemmas.

Related to a branch of psychology known as behaviorism, rationalist theories have a simple view of the human mind as oriented to external rewards (they explicitly opposed Freudian theories that focused on internal rewards). People are a bit like pigeons that can be trained to react to incentives without filtering information through their own minds. Nonetheless, rationalism made a contribution by demonstrating that purely self-interested individuals would not participate in protest, preferring to **free ride** on the efforts of others, since they would benefit if the effort succeeded without having to take any of the risks or pay any of the costs. (Rationalists have a narrow definition of self-interest.) This may help us understand why most people do not join social movements, even when they agree with the goals, but it also challenges us to understand the cultural and psychological work that *does* draw people into protest.

In addition to rational choice theory, plausible versions of psychological theories have survived which show how people compare themselves to other groups or to their own ideal to create moral ideologies that propel action. This **relative deprivation theory** sees culture as a source of comparisons. We can imagine how life *could* be, and find the present wanting: why should the richest 1 percent of Americans own 43 percent of the country's wealth? Are they really that much better than we are? When people make comparisons at the group level, they are especially likely to grow indignant – on behalf of their group.

By positing fairly universal psychological processes, lodged in the individual brain and personality, most psychological theories ignore cultural dynamics: all nuclear families are wracked by oedipal dynamics, all individuals feel alienated when they lack clear social and economic roles in their society, all individuals attempt to maximize their incomes and wealth. In the mysterious leap from individual feelings to large-scale politics, cultural understandings and expectations are left out. I may be hungrier when I am laid off from work, but I don't automatically go out and start throwing stones. I need to understand my situation as shared with many other people, and I need to blame state and corporate decisions rather than bad luck or uncontrollable market forces. I may start off angry, but that anger can either turn outward and grow into moral indignation or it can turn inward and lapse into resignation and depression. And that depends on social networks, protest groups, moral entrepreneurs, resources, and more: both

27

cultural and structural factors working together to lead from psychology to action.

Structural theories displaced psychological theories in the 1970s as the prevalent way to understand social movements; they suggest that institutional constraints will force action down certain paths regardless of how protestors feel and think about the world. All the mental-emotional activities central to psychological models were abandoned. The structural constraints are often resources: if a state goes bankrupt, revolution will usher in a new, more effective regime. But they also include coercive capacity: if the army is defeated in a war, and too disorganized to repress protestors at home, revolution can succeed.

Structural theories conveniently assume that there is always enough discontent in a population that, given the opportunity (for example, the prospect of not being slaughtered), people will mobilize together. They tend to define movements as composed of outsiders or **challengers** who wish to become **members** with voting and other political rights; Wilkes's followers are a good example. Structural theories tend to have a "lock-and-key" model of protest: choosing the right strategy will open the door to the political structures.

Resources are so important to every organization that an entire structural theory of social movements arose in the late 1970s called **resource mobilization theory**. Its proponents, John McCarthy and Mayer Zald (1977) suggested all sorts of ways that the search for funds shapes what **social movement organizations** (they called them SMOs) do. They act differently if they are competing with other organizations for the same donations, if they have a small or a large number of donors, or if they are asking people to donate who are not directly affected by the issue but are merely sympathetic. SMOs are shaped by their need for money, without which they would fail.

Following their provocative economic metaphor, that movement organizations are like firms competing in a market for attention and money, McCarthy and Zald suggested that **moral entrepreneurs** might invest some of their own money in starting a protest group, and then go out and try to persuade others that this new cause is worth supporting. McCarthy and Zald's ideas remain relevant today, although it turns out that not all protest groups are interested in building up the professional and financial infrastructure of a formal organization. Not every environmental group aspires to be the Sierra Club or Greenpeace. When they do, relying on supporters for nothing more than an annual donation, they are usually called interest groups instead of protest groups or social movements.

Another structural theory emerged which focused on political opportunities instead of resources (McAdam 1982; Tarrow 1998). Known as **political process** or **political opportunity theory**, it concentrates on structural openings in the **polity**, which consists of both political institutions and the elites who control them. When elites disagree among themselves, one faction may open the door to non-elites to enter the political system in order to create new allies. Or political elites may lose the means (money or military power) to suppress other groups.

Resource mobilization and political opportunity theories dovetailed nicely and eventually merged into one theory: how wealthy or well connected a group is affects what opportunities are open to it. Movements that are composed of poor people, such as welfare recipients or unemployed workers, will have a harder time accumulating the money for a large office and professional staff than a movement that appeals to the middle class, such as many wildlife or environmental groups. Building up their organization may simply not be an option for poor people's movements, so they may be better off concentrating on amassing large numbers of their members (something they *do* have) and shutting down businesses or governments. Or they may need to find allies with political power or money who are sympathetic to their cause (elite allies are central to both these theories).

Resource mobilization theories focus on money, political opportunity theories focus on coercion by the state. But persuasion is the heart of social movements, and neither theory – being structural – offers much insight into persuasion. Persuasion is linked to morality: we persuade someone to do something, most of the time, because it is right. No one thinks that payments or coercion are inherently moral, although they need to be justified on moral grounds (persuasion, again). But in and of themselves, they even have a whiff of immorality to them. We don't feel that people should have to be paid or coerced to do what is right.

These two theories concentrate on the means but ignore the motivations for protest. Originally they were rejecting simplified psychological theories, but as newer cultural theories appeared they have been able to incorporate some cultural dynamics. Up to a point: one of the founders of political opportunity theory, Doug McAdam, was quoted in a newspaper article about Occupy Wall Street: "Successful movements start out as expressions of anger, and then quickly move beyond that." This theoretical tradition no longer denies emotions – in fact, McAdam acknowledges their centrality here, but he just as quickly says that movements move on to more important things, presumably building organizations and networks, developing cognitive frames and media-friendly stories, and engaging politicians. But much of the subsequent work that movements do builds on that anger, crafts symbols which embody it, uses it to recruit and motivate continued mobilization. Anger does not disappear.

There is culture hidden in even the most structural models. Instead of watching the money flow in traditional resource mobilization theory, we might ask why someone sympathizes with one cause rather than another. Or how a moral entrepreneur raises interest in her cause, and frames it in a way that attracts attention. Resources don't mobilize themselves: those with resources must be persuaded to part with them. And armies do not simply disappear after wartime defeat; before they refuse to put down protest, commanders and soldiers must lose faith in their ruler, sympathize with the protestors, or be angry at their own lack of pay (they often engage in their own protests). Psychological and structural theories were equally lopsided, in a dialogue of the deaf in which each ignored what the other highlighted.

Although structural and rationalist theories seem utterly different, one being concerned with large political structures and the other with individuals, they look similar from a cultural perspective, since structural theories only work if they assume something about how individuals operate that looks a lot like the suppositions of rational choice theory. Structures only determine how people in them will act if we can assume that they always maximize something like income or power (more complicated psychological processes and motivations are ruled out). Structural theories need rationalist theories. But if people make different kinds of choices, based on their complex moral visions and cultural understandings, then both rationalist and structuralist approaches are limited in what they can explain. That is why both structural theorists (McAdam et al. 2001) and rationalist theorists (Opp 2009) have tried to incorporate culture into their models in recent years; the result is that there are few purely structural or rationalist theories left anymore.

Another kind of theory turns to history to explain protest, finding stages that somehow inevitably follow one another. **Historical theories** can take either structural or more cultural forms. Marx promoted the former approach with his idea that, just as capitalism had replaced feudal society, so socialism and later communism must violently overthrow capitalism. Culture is irrelevant because the strict laws of capitalism mean that most people will eventually become so impoverished and miserable that they will happily join the revolution, and capitalist business cycles will grow so extreme that the entire system must collapse one day. Complacent workers will be forced to set aside their "false consciousness" in favor of an accurate view of capitalist reality and the new socialist alternative. Marx's primary model was especially mechanistic (and structural), as he believed he had discovered the iron laws of historical development, driven ultimately by changes in the technologies of production. This does not leave much for organizers and workers to do, which is one reason Marxism has always been more popular with intellectuals than with the working class it aimed at. Today its main contribution is to remind us how extensively corporations intervene to manipulate markets and to corrupt political arenas.

Marx's idea that there are stages of history has inspired other historical models that take cultural meanings more seriously but which also claim to know the direction in which history is moving. The French scholar Alain Touraine (1981) suggested that the struggle over material production that dominated industrial society would be replaced by a struggle over symbolic understandings in a "postindustrial society" where universities, the media, and other symbol-makers are more and more important. Instead of capital versus labor, the core conflict for industrial society, the central struggle would now be between **technocrats** (bureaucrats in both corporations and the state) and **new social movements** for democracy, such as students, feminists, and ecologists.

Although Touraine insisted on the importance of culture, especially collective identities, the meanings he offered came from his own interpretation of history rather than from the meanings that protestors themselves attach to their actions. This was a problem, as movements followed their own ideas, not his. Contrary to Touraine's theory, there is no reason to assume that every society must have one dominant struggle; the great anti-technocratic movement never emerged out of all these different specific movements.

Other Big Theories of History have pitted modernism against postmodernism, or colonial versus postcolonial versus post-postcolonial (Dabashi 2012). Historical theories not only claim to find moments when "everything changed," but also to uncover the hidden "real meaning" of a movement in relation to history. Like Touraine, they are not cultural theories, strictly speaking, since they impose their own meaning (or history's supposed meaning) on the protestors they study.

Tilly's version of political opportunity theory, heavily influenced by Marx, combined historical and structural traditions. Modernization brought with it a package of institutional transformations: capitalism and a strong nation-state, foremost, but also accountable legislatures, national media, improved transportation, enormous cities, professional police forces – all of which changed protest in the direction of national organizations, especially unions, and a desire to influence legislation. We saw this trend beginning with "Wilkes and Liberty." Like other structuralists Tilly (2008) eventually came to recognize that cultural processes of persuasion are also a central part of the story.

That brings us to cultural theories. Since you will find pieces of them throughout the book, including framing, narrative, and emotion theories, I will not describe them here. But I want to point to a close relative, social psychology. This is a lively field of its own, which has contributed greatly to the cultural understanding of protest (Klandermans 1997; Pinard 2011). It overcomes the individualism of older psychological approaches by placing the individual's attitudes and emotions in social context, in interaction with others, but it falls a bit short of a full cultural perspective by restricting itself mostly to the mental processes and products of individuals through surveys and experiments. A full cultural approach observes people in their natural settings.

From structure to action

Big structural and historical theories promise more than we can really know. There are events that change a lot of things, but never everything. And we can know the direction of these changes only later, with hindsight. History itself never cooperates with big theories like these. We can know more about things that have already happened, and we can know more about small, observable things than about big unobservable things like "history" or "society" as a system.

This means that we can better explain what happens – why a movement emerges when it does, or why it has the impact it does – by putting together a long series of **causal mechanisms** at an observable, micro-social level of individuals and their interactions. An activist persuades her neighbor to attend a rally; the rally creates a good mood, and many participants devote more time to the cause; one of them writes a letter to his friend, a city council member, who in turn holds a public hearing, which attracts a news reporter, and so on. We follow a number of individuals, who do a variety of things each day, who react to each other with a tangle of feelings, who listen to and interpret others. Put enough of these little interactions together, and you have politics. A mechanisms approach is the opposite of historical theories, and

33

it can incorporate culture in a more thorough way by examining the perspectives of individuals and small groups.

A mechanisms approach can incorporate more than culture. Each of the non-cultural theories has some truth to it. Instead of seeing them as distinct theories, which we could try to compare to each other, we can transform the insights of each into mechanisms. There are psychological mechanisms such as emotions, structural mechanisms like resources and the rules of arenas, historical mechanisms like the differences between modern and premodern cities and media, and rationalist mechanisms like the pursuit of goals. All these factors help us understand protest, but we need to put them together. In this way, by making them into mechanisms (or variables), we can pull together the kernels of truth in all these theories.

Theories necessarily take real human beings and reduce them to caricatures, but some theories do this more than others. A micro-level cultural approach does it less, because it acknowledges their point of view, their sense of themselves as humans, facing choices and engaging with others. More structural approaches ignore these cultural and psychological processes. Micro-level approaches are theories of action, not of structure.

Sociological explanations always include both action and the constraints on action, and this book is no exception. One problem with structural theories is that they focus on one particular kind of constraint, namely those imposed by resources and arenas. They overlook the constraints imposed by other players, who are pursuing their own strategies, making their own decisions, and often trying hard to block the initiatives of protestors. So it is worth taking time to look at the components of action. It's a focus on action – and the culture that shapes it – that makes a theory humanistic, respecting the people we study even when we dislike or disagree with them.

All actions are physical. That sounds silly, but we need to look at the ways in which action is *embodied*: how it feels to someone, how it looks to others, the limits of what a body can do, and how two individuals do the "same" thing in slightly different ways. Our bodies are not the only physical aspect of action; we act in particular *places*, which become arenas when we carry out political activity in them. Wilkes made the street into an arena. Most arenas already have various expectations and traditions, various physical possibilities and impossibilities, but strategic players always try to expand what is possible for themselves and limit it for their opponents. It may seem obvious, but we will see all sorts of ways that places and bodies shape political action.

Action may be physical but it is also based on *meanings*: we understand what we are doing, and we attribute meaning to what others do as well. (What we think they are doing and what they think they are doing may not entirely coincide, especially since strategic players often try to deceive each other.) These meanings may change and emerge during the actions themselves, and there are conflicts over what those meanings are. The King saw Wilkes as a criminal, subject to prosecution for treason, but his supporters insisted he was a freeborn Englishman exercising his rights, a symbol of liberty – a view that eventually won out. Wilkes inspired commoners, gave them hope for change, and made them angry at his prosecution. They felt their way to a social movement; they were not following some philosopher's blueprint. They tried assorted tactics, looking for any that would work.

We are not fully conscious of every meaning we hold. That would paralyze us. We are implicitly aware of all sorts of things that we do not need to stop and think about explicitly. We use our senses and our emotions to do a great deal of our thinking for us, processing information about what is happening around us, telling us whether we need to pay closer attention, helping us begin to formulate a response. An affective commitment like trust allows us to side with comrades in an argument without having to calculate whether we necessarily agree with their position. Subconscious thinking sometimes leads us to make mistakes (just as conscious thinking does), but when we realize this we usually adjust our thinking as a result.

Action brings people and *objects* together: banners, clothes, barricades, tear gas, journalists, police officers, and protestors add up to a demonstration. In Wilkes's era, wealthy supporters treated the crowds to rounds of alcohol, which warmed them up and gave them an added incentive to show up. Resources useful for today's protestors are more likely to be mass mailings, brochures, and websites, but the key insight of resource mobilization theory holds true: protestors have more options when they have more money.

There are hundreds of actions available to protestors, but they tend to stick to a small number of familiar activities. Tilly dubbed this the **repertory** shared by different movements in a given country in a given period, for in his long historical perspective he could see how much these had changed in the modern world. New protests follow existing repertories for several reasons. Activists have the know-how to pull it off, partly because individuals move from one movement to another, bringing their personal knowledge with them. Plus, if a tactic is familiar, it probably has some moral legitimacy; audiences are unlikely to be outraged into a backlash against the protest. Finally, some actions are easier than others, given the available arenas and resources. A class-action lawsuit is plausible only in a system open to suits by class-action lawyers; otherwise, only the wealthy can hire lawyers and pursue legal strategies. If protestors see arenas as fixed, with only one way to open them, they will search for that key. This is why Tilly also embraced the concept of political opportunities: repertories and arenas develop over time through repeated interactions. Protestors abandon tactics that do not fit the arenas they face, and embrace those that do. They find the right keys to open the available locks.

Tactical choices are also subject to a kind of natural selection process: the more different tactics that a group tries, the more likely it is to find one that works. But it does not try things randomly; activists constantly assess the strengths and weaknesses of their opponents, trying to identify tactics that will take advantage of those weak spots: the right key. Wilkes recognized that King George was vulnerable on the issues of arrogance and corruption.

The weakness of the lock-and-key model is that the political system and other targets do not sit still and wait for protestors to try their keys; they anticipate what protestors will do and try to block them. So the opportunities are always shifting, because of players' expectations and actions. Each player tries to guess what the other players will do next. Political action is always *interaction*: it is an engagement between two or more players over something they all care about.

Protestors do not simply look around for the right key. As Wilkes's case shows, they also invent new tactics, taking advantage of changing arenas or inventing new ones. The creativity of action is exciting but hard to predict, and scholars have done a poor job of explaining it. A creative move often emerges when the normal moves are blocked, although the result can also just be a desperate move. Sometimes desperate moves succeed. Individuals are also a part of creativity, since they frequently combine different kinds of information or points of view of a problem. A newcomer can often see the whole situation differently.

Protest would be easy if there were always one right thing to do in every situation. But there are always many things to do, and often none of them is especially good. Strategic action is full of dilemmas and compromises: each option is promising in some ways, but risky in others. Protestors do not always recognize the dilemmas they face; they do not realize they could do something different. They rely on familiar routines. But even when they do not acknowledge a dilemma, it is still lurking there, as a trade-off. There are hidden alternatives. In many cases, there is a good reason an option is ignored: it is just too costly. But sometimes, the blinders of the existing repertory prevent the full range of options from being considered. It is always easiest to rely on familiar tactics. This is when a creative change is possible, when someone suddenly sees the tradeoff as a **choice point**, when there are two or more different options, generating the possibility to do something different.

Emotions would seem to be a long way from the world of strategic calculation, but they play a role in all choices. We avoid some choices out of fear, or because they make us morally uneasy, as in the dirty-hands dilemma. Positive feelings toward a group or individual – such as trust or admiration – lead us to embrace tactics that we associate with them. Just as protest organizers try to arouse emotions of pride, joy, and compassion in participants, so opponents try to inculcate resignation, depression, shame, fatigue, and fear. We feel our way to decisions more than we calculate. Like our thoughts, most of our emotions operate beneath consciousness.

* * *

In the last 250 years, more and more protest has taken the form of social movements, with repertories focused on persuasion. Wilkes and other figures have invented new forms of action in the face of new resources, opportunities, and meanings. Some theories focus on historical and structural shifts, others on individual psychology. But almost all theories of social movements have come to acknowledge that cultural meanings deserve a place in their explanations.

Just as scholars explain action by interpreting what all the players think they are doing, what they are expecting, hoping, and desiring, so the players themselves interpret what everyone else is doing. They watch, they listen, they try to put themselves inside the heads of opponents or bystanders. This is as true of politicians, corporate executives, and police officers as it is of protestors. They interpret each other's words and actions, and respond in the way they think best. They even watch and interpret their *own* actions, occasionally surprising themselves by grasping consciously what they had only known intuitively before. This kind of interpretation is the heart of culture; it is through interpretation that we constantly impose meaning on the world. But what are the mechanisms with which we do this? What carries our meanings?

2

Meaning

One becomes woman: the feminist movement

In the UK and the US the women's movement has persisted through long periods of quiet, punctuated by occasional waves of activity. In Britain, polite mobilization for suffrage accelerated after 1905 into street demonstrations, arson, window-smashing, and, in 1909, hunger strikes, to which the government responded with forced feeding, a gruesome and often scarring procedure. (The same government allowed Irish nationalist prisoners in the same period to starve to death.) In a unique form of protest, the suffragists also slashed paintings in art galleries. British women (if they were at least 30 years old and owned property) received the right to vote in 1918, American women in 1920. Britain's restrictions were removed in 1928.

American women took the lead in the 1960s, with two related waves of activity based on distinct but overlapping networks. An older group, mostly professionals who favored changes in laws, contributed to, but were also reinvigorated by, President Kennedy's commission on women of 1963. Their work led to equal employment opportunity legislation and then a flood of lawsuits, followed – when those complaints were not taken seriously by the new Equal Employment Opportunity Commission – by the formation of the National Organization for Women (NOW) in 1966. In the late 1960s a younger group of women, who had been activists in the civil rights and student movements but who felt blocked and even ridiculed by the men who dominated these movements, began to form protest and consciousness-raising groups.

The younger, more radical movement was reacting to the larger society's sexism, but also to the supposedly radical men with whom they had worked well for years until the women began asking for their own rights. They were also criticizing NOW's liberal version of feminism, expressed in Betty Friedan's *The Feminine Mystique* (1963), which demanded women's greater participation in the economic and political institutions of modern America without questioning the prevailing dichotomy of private versus public. Women were supposed to run corporations but also do all the cooking and diapers at home. The radicals famously insisted, "The personal is political." Sexism permeates every interaction, even the most intimate, between men and women; the dichotomy of male and female imposes itself on every young person.

A number of these women, who had devoted years to radical politics, shared the same shock when they asked that attention be paid to sexism. For example, when 2,000 anti-war and civil rights activists from more than 200 groups converged for a conference in August 1967, hoping to unite the American left, an informal women's caucus tried to submit a resolution in favor of women's rights. They were blocked, first by the resolutions committee and then on the floor of the convention (even though they had been promised they would be able to speak). They were simply refused the microphone. In response, "Shulie Firestone and about 3 or 4 other people . . . were ready to pull the place apart. Then William Pepper [a prominent civil rights attorney] patted Shulie on the head and said, 'Move on little girl; we have more important issues to talk about here than women's liberation'" (quoted in Evans 1979: 198–9). From their furious frustration came an influential manifesto and a network of devoted, indignant feminists.

These women knew how to mobilize people, thanks to their training in the other movements of the 1960s. They launched hundreds of consciousness-raising groups, a new setting in which women shared stories of sexism, both large and small. In these sheltered spaces they worked out many analyses of how cultural meanings operated, especially by attacking a series of dichotomies related to male–female (active–passive, mind–body, thinking–feeling, and so on). And yet they began not with the kind of grand ideologies beloved by many men of the New Left, but by sharing their feelings, their suppressed anger and shame. Individuals came to realize that their own disappointments and mistreatment were shared by many, even millions of, other women. They felt their way to a new realization that womanhood is a cultural construction not a biological imperative. They rediscovered Simone de Beauvoir's *The Second Sex*, in which she wrote: "One is not born, but rather becomes woman: no biological, psychological, or economic fate determines the figure that the human female presents in society" (2010 [1949]: 267).

Women activists – especially white, middle-class women – had to learn how to be angry. Or at least how to express their anger politically rather than bottling it up inside. Anger, and especially its moral form of indignation, are necessary for protesting against injustice and demanding one's due as a human being, which is exactly the reason that subordinate groups such as women are usually trained not to display anger. Feminists learned to show how angry they were. One participant recalls the contrast between the joy and humor of private meetings and the serious anger displayed at public meetings. "Rape and domestic violence weren't funny, nor was sexual harassment. Male jokes about feminist goals only deepened activists' anger" (Rosen 2000: 220). Indignation must be enacted publicly, and laughter might undermine it.

Internal and external pressures suppressed the US women's movement in the 1980s. Differences of sexual orientation and race-ethnicity fractured the supposedly unified identity of women, as did disagreements over issues like pornography. In the political arena, the Christian Right (see chapter 3) began to resist and even roll back some of women's gains, blocking the Equal Rights Amendment and chipping away at abortion rights. Moderate legal strategies continued, steadily but slowly, to promote equality in the workplace, but most radical agendas faltered. The very term "feminist" was attacked, and what had been a proud label for many women became, for their daughters, a quaint or irrelevant

41

anachronism – or worse. And yet feminists left behind broad changes in what people think women are like and can do.

Feminism will show us how cultural meanings are packaged, reinforced, and conveyed to new audiences. As I said, I adopt a broadly rhetorical approach to understanding how humans impose meaning on the world around us and express how we think and feel to others. We must always pay attention to who creates the meanings, how they are embodied, and who the audiences are, as Aristotle observed. Rhetoric is an evocative way to think about the role of culture in politics, because it emphasizes that people have goals, that they are audiences for each other's words and actions, and thus they interpret information. Rhetoric also involves emotions, because they are the reason that something has meaning for us.

Physical carriers

Meanings don't just float in the air around us. They take physical forms, and there is an infinite number of forms they can take. Almost anything can be used to convey meanings: sermons, letters, advertisements; frescoes, paintings, and stained-glass windows; rituals, parades, and other actions; as well as words in a book, newspaper, or website. We even attribute meaning to things we didn't create, like mountains or seas, which we nonetheless appropriate as convenient symbols.

Words are the most common carriers, uttered first in conversations among intimates. Jokes and snide remarks, no doubt as old as language, are a mild form of protest, hidden transcripts that allow those who hear them some sense that not everyone accepts the current arrangements or admires those who benefit from them. Sustained discussions can make explicit all the criticism that jokes merely suggest. Widening the circle, orators can address thousands in a speech, which can only occur once bigger arenas for persuasion have been imagined and built.

Once languages are written, new media allow words to be saved over time and carried across distances. At first only elites could read, and they used written language for their own purposes (especially keeping track of who had paid their debts and taxes), but as literacy spread so did the written word's capacity to mobilize people. As the media became cheaper – as the printing press replaced scribes, as cheap newsprint replaced rags – more people could afford to buy printed versions of arguments, even though these have always been supplemented by oral discussions. Today, the cheap costs and broad reach of the mass media make them the ideal means of communicating meanings, which is why protestors work so hard to gain news coverage.

Naming is an important use of words because a name suggests a whole way of seeing a phenomenon, or of seeing something we have not noticed before. "Sexism," like racism or speciesism or inequality, connotes a problematic attitude as well as a group of victims. "Post-traumatic stress disorder" puts the blame for mental illness on war experiences rather than on veterans themselves. Naming a social problem is an important step toward addressing it.

The names of protest groups and movements are also important, since they sum up a group's identity, purpose, even moral tone. They can have historical resonance, like Redstockings, or be playful like the magazine *Spare Rib*. They can be pugnacious, such as the Virago Press, or earnest and serious, like the New York Radical Women. Or they can suggest a broad collective identity, such as the National Organization for Women. They help define these players.

The women's movement turned especially to poets, specialists in words, to help it articulate the new sensibility emerging from the consciousness-raising groups. Feminists paid close attention to the sexism in our language. Poetry is also adept at probing emotions, and at showing the relationship between public and private experience. Short poems are also easy to read – and maybe to write – in women's busy schedules, according to Audre Lorde: "poetry can be done between shifts, on the subway, on scraps of surplus paper" (quoted in Reed 2005: 93).

Visual forms have accompanied verbal forms of meaning almost from the start, as we gather from cave carvings that are up to

300,000 years old. Like the physical carriers of words, those for images have changed enormously. Some means are the same for words and images: printing gave us the art of engraving; cheap newsprint offered lithographs; glossy paper allowed magazines to print photographs. Through most of recorded history, rulers used images to convey their messages of power and inevitability, dotting the landscape with their own images.

Protestors appreciate that those same images of power can be distorted to deliver the opposite message, through graffiti, the occasional Hitler moustache on a poster, and other quick adaptations. The built environment offers innumerable spots for political images. For example, Occupy Wall Street had a truck that could project anti-capitalist messages onto the sides of enormous buildings, temporary billboards visible to thousands.

Today, moving images are so cheap that protests are fed live to the internet, available around the world. Live-streamers accompanied every Occupy event, despite frequent interference and arrests by police who recognized that nothing could get them in trouble faster than being caught on video harassing or pushing, much less striking, a peaceful demonstrator. Vlad Teichberg, who organized much of Occupy's live streaming, says that it "creates an instantaneous eye that cannot be censored. It is one of the most honest forms of journalism because you can't even go back and edit yourself." On the other hand, editing yourself is often helpful.

Visual images have their own iconography, the pictorial equivalent of the vocabularies that give meaning to words. Some images suggest strength or weakness: someone drawn in the shape of a horse or an elephant, or as a mouse or bird. A large size or large muscles also suggest strength. Other images connote moral qualities: an evil person is shown with fangs or horns, squinting eyes, pointed ears; a kindly figure with a calm smile, upright posture, reassuring gestures. From ingredients like these protest movements create heroes, villains, and victims. As the old expression about a thousand words suggests, a visual image such as a caricature can immediately convey qualities about a person; we automatically develop good or bad feelings from these carefully crafted pictures.

Books are primarily devoted to words, but they often contain

Even leftist politicians like Jean-Luc Mélenchon are not exempt from Hitler moustaches (2012 French presidential campaign). Credit: JMJ.

images as well. They are important to most protest movements, as they are cheap, can be hidden or transported easily, and pack extensive detail – both evidence and argument – into a small space, all of which is equally true of their new electronic versions. (You would not be reading this if I didn't think books were an effective rhetorical device.) Several books have become almost sacred texts to social movements: Harriet Beecher Stowe's *Uncle Tom's Cabin* to nineteenth-century abolitionists; Rachel Carson's *Silent Spring* to environmentalists; Peter Singer's *Animal Liberation* to animal rights activists; and of course Betty Friedan's *The Feminine Mystique* to the women's movement.

More protestors refer to these books than have actually read them, suggesting that they have a symbolic purpose beyond the spread of information. They lend a movement intellectual respectability, and suggest that there is hard evidence behind its claims.

A big book often includes the heroic story of one person's conversion to the cause, suggesting that anyone who looked at the evidence closely would do the same thing. Betty Friedan presented herself as a discontented housewife from middle America, hiding her history as a leftwing journalist, especially for the Communist-led United Electrical, Radio, and Machine Workers of America. But discontented housewives were her target audience, and the first paperback edition of her book sold a gargantuan 1.4 million copies. Subsequent feminists could point to this book as an inspiration, whether or not they had read it (Coontz 2011).

Activists often point to a big book as the source of their movement, implying that the author just couldn't take it anymore, but in fact big books often emerge from an incipient movement and then become bestsellers because of the growth of the movement (Meyer and Rohlinger 2012). Meanings and mobilization influence each other. Books don't create movements by themselves.

Graffiti take anonymous advantage of visible public spaces to convey a brief message. A graffito (singular for graffiti) may include images as well as words, or simple icons that combine the two. At their most elaborate, graffiti blossom into *murals*, entire walls transformed into political messages. In the US, Chicano militants adapted the Mexican mural tradition to their own neighborhoods, celebrating heroes and condemning daily discriminations. Just as graffiti exploit public places, they also transform the messages already found there, especially advertisements that can be ridiculed or subverted with a simple letter or word added, an eye or tooth blacked out. The most memorable graffiti usually evoke a laugh. On the other hand, even though scholars celebrate graffiti as grassroots resistance, much of it never rises above the narcissistic vandalism of personal "tags."

Music is another ancient form that still has a central role in protest. For one thing, it conveys messages through lyrics, pithy summaries of political visions (Eyerman and Jamison 1998). But music does something that is even more powerful: it absorbs the entire body in ways that can put people in ecstatic moods. Singing together – along with dancing, marching, praying, and laughing – gives people a feeling of mutual solidarity that words and images alone cannot (Rosenthal and Flacks 2012). Coordinated motion, which usually requires music to guide it, makes people feel as though they are part of a much larger body – in what sociologist Émile Durkheim called **collective effervescence**. This joyful mood is the central pleasure that encourages participants to return to future events.

Performing arts like dance or theater utilize a fourth kind of vocabulary, in which bodies and motion express various meanings. These include facial expressions and gestures as well as more sweeping dance steps, all of which convey human situations in ways not available through words, still images, or music – even though these forms are often woven together in performances. Activists "choreograph" their events, directing who moves when and where, even if they are unaware of the exact language of the performing arts. Street theater has been a standard part of the protest repertory for thousands of years. Live performances are equally important for their *gathering* function of assembling people: hundreds or thousands of potential recruits will come to hear a concert or a good speech, but leave feeling part of a protest movement.

The *human body* also carries meanings, especially but not only in performances. Or rather, we are always performing to some extent. Our postures, our gestures, the look in our eyes, all "speak" to our audiences. Perhaps the most effective cultural medium of all is the human voice, which, through changes in timbre and tempo, can suggest every sort of emotion, can convey urgency, and can color every word or fact (to the point of undermining the very words it states even while stating them).

One special kind of performance is the wearing of *masks* or *costumes*. These convey messages without the wearer doing much at all, although they can be combined with words or elaborate dramas. A recent example shows how old images can be charged with new meanings. The Guy Fawkes mask, used in the UK to commemorate the failure of a Catholic attempt to blow up parliament in 1605, was taken up in comic books and then a 2006 movie, *V for Vendetta*, as an anarchist symbol of resistance to the corporate corruption of politics. The group Anonymous likes it for hiding individuals while accenting the solidarity of the group. In 2012 a

Meaning

A familiar anti-corporate performance. Credit: Haeferi, Wikimedia Commons.

group of Polish legislators even used the mask to show their disapproval of a neoliberal treaty against trade in counterfeit goods.

Our *built environment* also conveys cultural meanings. Some buildings help create players. Corporate headquarters, government ministries, and countercultural coffeehouses all send messages about the organizations or subcultures housed in them. Other buildings contain strategic arenas. Think of courtrooms, with raised benches, flags, railings, and decorations, all intended to suggest the calm justice of the law or the power of the state, reinforced by the costumes, stylized arguments, and ritual actions that occur there. Wise words from our founders are chiseled into marble walls to guide future actions. Buildings are not the only carriers that we erect: highways, gardens, parks, airports and train stations, monuments and memorials, cemeteries, and more, all shape how we feel and think about the world.

Different media suggest meaning in different ways, and

combinations of several forms probably get the message across most effectively. A movement's activists may be particularly gifted in one medium, for instance attracting musicians or graphic artists, but most movements deploy words, images, music, and sometimes performances. You never know which physical carrier is going to reach an individual, so you try as many as you can afford.

But the creation of art is not always just a cost: art can be sold to finance a cause. The most extreme cases involve concerts that raise millions for musicians' favorite causes, but posters, books, and any other objects can be sold by movement groups. There is another way in which art is not a cost: people enjoy making it. Groups enjoy coming together to play music, build floats, or create giant puppets.

There are other variations in the production, distribution, and consumption of meaning objects. In some cases, the creators and the audiences of cultural media are present at the same time, allowing feedback and interaction between the two; at other times the two are separated in space and/or time. Some cultural artifacts last a long time once they are created, allowing future generations to contemplate and interpret them; others disappear upon their creation, such as live performances. Some cultural products, in addition, can be mass-produced or broadcast, while others are unique. These differences all affect how a movement conveys its vision of the world.

Figurative carriers

We have seen a variety of physical carriers of meaning, but the messages they convey are also bundled together in many different *figurative* forms that are meant to grab attention and have an impact on audiences. Through figures like these, cultural meanings rise from mere *intelligibility* (I understand the words "pepper spray") to *resonance* (I become nervous as I appreciate what pepper spray feels like, and that an officer with it is walking in my direction). For a meaning to resonate, it must engage our feelings and not simply trigger a dictionary definition in our heads. I list some figurative carriers in table 2.

Meaning

Table 2 Figurative carriers of meanings

Maxims and proverbs	Pithy formulations shape our common sense
Jokes	An aggressive tone can be turned toward the power-ful, often to devastating effect on reputations
Slogans and chants	As brief as maxims, these are often created by pro-testors to present a political diagnosis and a plea for action
Frames	A kind of underlying metaphor that includes diagnosis of a problem, suggests solutions, and hopefully moti-vates action
Collective identities	We come to feel part of a group, cognitively, emo-tionally, and morally, and are willing to take action on its behalf
Characters	Heroes, villains, victims, and minions are components of identities that carry with them moral judgment and suggest the emotions we are supposed to feel toward these players
Narratives	Stories have characters who do things to one another, a plot that pulls these actions together, a sense of time that links successive actions, a beginning, middle, and end, and some kind of moral or judgment
Facts	Supposedly simple claims about reality are embedded in narratives, frames, and character work, giving them greater plausibility. Sometimes the facts are supposed to "stand on their own"
Rules and laws	Instructions about how to act, these are also sym-bolic statements about what is normal and moral
Ideologies	Elaborate systems of ideas, identities, stories, frames, slogans, facts, and other elements, they are meant to both explain the world and suggest action

Concise maxims, jokes, and slogans work because they connote so much in a few memorable words or images. Often these sayings are ways of summing up other people's characters: "A coward is a hero with a wife, kids, and a mortgage." Many proverbs have a cynical edge that excuses inaction – still an important part of any explanation of politics, since most people most of the time do *not* get involved. They stand on the sidelines and make snide comments.

Certain formulas, based on the rhythms of poetry, are easily recycled: "Women, united, will never be defeated!" Or this effort to link sexism to violence: "2, 4, 6, 8; stop the violence, stop the rape!" As drill sergeants know, alternations between stressed and unstressed syllables are easy to march to. Song lyrics tend to be more complex, but they too must be catchy enough to sing and simple enough to remember. Slogans are meant to appear on a banner or an advertisement, but chants need to fully engage the bodies of marchers in ways that generate energy and joy.

Frames are more complex. "Rape as violence" suggests a number of claims about sexism, women's status as objects, and the inadequacies of a criminal justice system that instead sees "rape as sex." "Pornography is the theory, rape the practice" implicates what had merely been dirty magazines or movies in a system of violence against women. Frames were one of the first tools that scholars developed for thinking about cultural meanings in protest, and hundreds of studies have examined the frames deployed by every sort of social movement (Snow et al. 1986; Benford 1997).

If frames tend to diagnose the problems that need to be fixed, collective identities suggest the group that is supposed to fix them. In many cases the group is already defined by shared experiences, treatment, or structural position: laws may discriminate against them, stereotypes demean them. They may be prohibited from voting. Some of the greatest movements in history spoke in the name of second-class citizens, such as the Wilkes agitation, the US civil rights movement, and of course the women's movement, which at the beginning of the twentieth century pursued suffrage in most countries but by the end of the century was fighting workplace harassment, pay discrimination, glass ceilings, and demeaning media images. Feminists tried to persuade members of the group that "all women" shared the same problems and needed the same solutions.

Stories seduce us into going along with their characterizations and their moral judgments because they deploy the full range of human passions. They also come in an infinite variety of versions, which can be tailored to fit the audiences in different arenas (Polletta 2006).

Meaning

Some stories are grand theories of history: in primitive groups men and women were once equal; with the rise of warfare and states women were excluded from power but still worked; under the influence of industrialization in the nineteenth century they were also pushed out of the workplace and into the home; thanks to the women's movement, they are beginning to assume positions of power in politics and the economy. Most protest stories depict the movement as the hero, saving individuals from oppression; most suggest that things are already getting better but have a long way to go. They also tend to insist on the urgency of political action: if only we act right now, things will improve; if we do not, they will get worse again.

Other stories are more local. They may concern the founding of a group, when a handful of good people found the courage to stand up for justice. Stories of individual courage are popular, like the prim and proper Rosa Parks, who refused to give up her bus seat to a white man in Montgomery, Alabama in 1955. Or the story of Betty Friedan, forlorn housewife who decided to write a book about her plight. In cases like these, we saw, individual heroes are emphasized, while their previous activism, organizational ties, and support networks are hidden from view. Individuals are good to think with, and good to feel with.

All these other figurative carriers imply that they are based on facts, and inevitably include some, and facts in turn gain plausibility from the broader carriers in which they are embedded. If I am moved by a narrative, I am more likely to believe the facts it contains; if I admire a character, I am more likely to believe complimentary facts about her. Most arguments contain apparently simple facts: American women earn 77 percent of what American men earn; there are no differences in average IQs of women and men. No fact is entirely objective; each comes with a history, assumptions built into it, definitions of the terms, and emotions surrounding it. But they have the aura of objective claims (they are framed as facts, we might say), and our opponents are always quick to try to dispute our facts.

If a movement lasts a while, and if it attracts writers and other intellectuals, they will eventually put these pieces together – identities,

52

stories, frames, and slogans – into an ideology (Fine 2012: ch. 5). Ideologies are often sloppy and always contain contradictions, with different *movement intellectuals* developing alternative versions. An ideology is reassuring to political activists because it usually suggests that history is on their side (and explains why it is), that their purposes are based on thorough evidence, and that large numbers of people share their view of the world. The broadest ideologies are part of mainstream politics – liberalism or socialism, for instance – but feminism, ecology, and other longstanding movements have developed their own ideologies over time, often through the work of engaged intellectuals (although some movements, such as Europe's autonomes or the Occupy movement, resist ideologies on the grounds that they become too rigid and constrain what activists can do and say).

Meanings always have a physical and a figurative dimension, both of which shape what we can and cannot understand about the world. One type of figure deserves special mention.

Political characters

Characters are key figurative meanings that arise in stories but also can be fashioned more directly through images, jokes, comments, arguments, and other physical and figurative carriers. The primary characters, reflecting their literary origins, are heroes, villains, and victims, who play out moral dramas of right and wrong. It is hard to create blame for a social problem without victims and villains, and it is helpful for social movements to position themselves as potential heroes. Moderate feminists singled out rapists and other violent men as the villains, but more extreme feminists portrayed anyone with a penis as a villain, and all women as victims, a view that discouraged alliances with men and eventually helped undermine the feminist movement in the 1980s.

Character work, intended to define their own and other players' character types, is central to protestors' rhetorical arsenals partly because characters tell us what emotions we are supposed to feel about them: we pity victims, we fear and hate villains, we

Table 3 Major (and some minor) characters

	Strong	Weak
Benevolent	Heroes	Victims
	Martyrs and saints (who start in cell	Sympathetic
	across)	bystanders
	Judges, donors	
	Converts (who start in cell below)	
	Friends	
Malevolent	Villains	Minions
	Outside agitators	Scoundrels
	Traitors (who start in cell above)	Cowardly bystanders
	Foes	

admire heroes, we feel contempt for minions. We also expect appropriate action from each character: heroes are supposed to defeat the villains and save the victims. Real people make the best characters, because it is easier to feel strongly about them than about abstractions, such as demographic categories. We may sympathize abstractly with "Southern black women," but Rosa Parks stirs our indignation as a victim and admiration as she transformed herself into a hero. And rhetorically, characters suggest a role for the audience: stop being a victim, and start acting like a hero.

Even in everyday life we size up the people we meet along two dimensions: are they good or bad, and are they strong or weak (Fiske 2012)? We want to know, perhaps instinctively, whether they intend to harm us, and whether they could do so if they wanted to. Even though we make those judgments in a fraction of a second, we rarely change our minds. First impressions matter, especially in politics, and so all players try to make a good one. These two dimensions define the basic character types in the table.

The most important characters for a movement to establish are the **victims,** for they show that there is some harm that needs to be fixed. Until judges and prosecutors viewed women beaten by their husbands as victims of domestic abuse, there was no crime to prosecute, no excuse for police to intervene, and little sense of public condemnation. Many social movements are all about establishing victims: of hazardous waste exposure, financial fraud, of corporate negligence, or biased media coverage. To name a victim is to name a problem or crime, and vice versa: glass ceilings have people who bump against them.

In a famous New York case that brought attention to domestic violence in 1987, photographs of Hedda Nussbaum's swollen, battered face made her a victim of her partner Joel Steinberg, instead of an accomplice in the death of their daughter Lisa. Images were more strikingly persuasive than the facts of the case, although lawyers, journalists, and antiviolence activists wove the two kinds of information together to establish one (male) villain and two (female) victims. (Had it come down to a conflict between the two victims, 6-year-old Lisa would have won; children make the most sympathetic victims.)

Once there is a victim, audiences look for a **villain**. If victims arouse compassion, villains stir up indignation. We seek humans to blame for the immoral choices they have made or continue to make. If we cannot find someone to blame for a problem, we tend to think of it as an act of God, or of nature, in which case we can still feel compassion for victims, but not indignation. If victims are supposed to look small, young, and innocent, villains are expected to look evil, with squinty eyes and unfriendly facial expressions. They must be menacing.

Heroes are supposed to fix the problem, typically by subduing the villains. Heroes are strong and good. This is normally an unstable combination, since we tend to fear those who are strong. So heroes are best when they are passive, sleeping giants, only moving into action when they are asked. Traditional heroes – and villains – were supernatural, and in Greek myths they were often (like the greatest of them, Heracles) the offspring of a god and a human. In the modern world, they have lost this aura of the divine, so mere mortals must step into the gap: normal people must band together to play the role of hero. Social movements are hardly divine, but by mobilizing large numbers of people they can set things right – and perhaps gain some sacred charisma. At least this is the rhetoric they commonly use to recruit and retain members.

"Together, we can do this." The "moral majority" must be roused to action.

The fourth cell in the table, containing weak and bad characters, is less populated. These are often referred to as **minions**, which implies small, ineffectual characters who are dangerous only when they have a villain to direct them. They are not a common rhetorical trope because, if you want to make someone appear threatening, you also want them to appear strong, a true villain. But you may instead wish to portray an opponent as weak and ridiculous, incapable of being a real threat. This dismissive approach can undermine support for a player, and may even lead them to doubt their own strength.

Authority figures are popular targets for minionhood. Protestors against the 2003 invasion of Iraq created a poster in which Vice-President Dick Cheney appeared as the gigantic Jabba the Hut from the *Star Wars* movies, with President George W. Bush as his tiny pet jester next to him, a minion on a leash with no will of his own. The rhetoric gains from the pairing of villain and minion, another example of a moral battery. (Also look at the image on page 165 in chapter 7.)

One of the most gripping stories that these characters can embody is that of a **conversion** from villain to hero: a whistle-blower or other insider, who used to be considered the enemy and knows a lot about the evil practices, decides that she was wrong and the protestors are right. The dark flipside is the betrayal of someone on your side who switches to the opposition, perhaps taking special knowledge with them. (Of course, they may have already been agents of the other side, spies gathering information.) One side's betrayal is the other side's heroism. I suggested earlier that protestors are modern-day heroes, but to their opponents – with opposite moral assumptions – they are villains or foolish minions.

Another sympathetic move is from victim to hero, someone who finally stands up to her oppressor. Abused children who grow into adult activists prefer terms like survivor, which suggests some of the strength of a hero, an accomplishment they can be proud of (Whittier 2011). They have the strength to fight back. **Martyrs**

Two dilemmas of character work

Protestors face dilemmas about how to portray themselves, but also how to describe their opponents. In particular, they must struggle over whether to portray themselves, or those they claim to represent, as victims or as heroes. Victims attract more sympathy, and perhaps financial donations, but they are also too weak to fight back, to mobilize a movement that can redress the wrongs. Heroes, on the other hand, may not need anyone's help.

When it comes to character work on your opponents, there is a similar dilemma over strength. If you portray them as villains, they are strong enough to hurt you, and you spread a sense of urgency in a social problem. But if you make them seem too strong, there may be little that can be done to fight them. Instead, you can ridicule them as clowns or minions, too weak to be much of a danger. Satire and mockery may discourage their supporters and undermine their self-confidence, and it may boost your own team's confidence. But how urgent is it to mobilize against them?

are a similar story of the weak and downtrodden revealing inner strength in sacrificing themselves. Moral strength can compensate for physical weakness.

Memory

A vivid field of study called **collective memory** has brought attention to the many ways that we commemorate, reinterpret, feel about, and build monuments to the past. People, events, and places from history hold meanings just as much as books or murals do. States have enormous advantages here as well as great interests at stake. They finance most monuments that celebrate battles and war deaths as well as the founding of the state itself. A great deal of collective memory is devoted to the histories of nations, and by

The innovation dilemma

Protestors try to change other people's view of the world, seducing them into a new moral vision, a new vocabulary of sympathy and suffering, new ways of feeling. Like artists, protestors push the boundaries of what can be thought, articulated, and felt. But how fast can they push these boundaries? Those already in a movement may be able to push the limits very far and fast, opening up new moral universes for themselves. But the greater the innovation, the more likely you are to lose your audience. You need to start where they are and bring them to where you are. Go too fast, and you lose them. Activists try to deal with this tension by finding just the right emblem of their vision: the inspiring individual (Rosa Parks), the horrid outrage (child abuse), the slogan that sums up many people's intuitive hopes and fears (the 99 percent). Protestors try to articulate what is already there. (The innovation dilemma applies to tactics as well as to cultural creations.)

implication of the states that rule them. The founding fathers must be portrayed as wise heroes who established legitimate organizations, not as radical revolutionaries who got their way through war or terror. Citizens are asked to respect the sacrifices that so many have made for the collective good. We fabricate special national stories, often referred to as **myths** when they come to be widely accepted.

These portrayals of history are often contested, and protestors sometimes discover that they disagree with some implication of a national myth. Should we really celebrate national heroes who owned slaves, beat their wives, or tortured captives during their war of liberation? Did they establish a political system without sufficient liberties for all citizens? Were they advancing their own economic interests? If heroes can be criticized for their failings in this way, one rhetorical alternative is to idolize the founders and attack their successors for not living up to the founding ideals or intents: Lenin would have shaped the USSR into a workers' paradise, but Stalin perverted it into a repressive bureaucratic state (according to Trotsky). Foundings are important components of national myths, frequently so popular that it is harder to question them than to keep them intact as grounds for criticizing recent deviations.

The field of collective memory reminds us that influential cultural meanings can be conveyed through the built environment. Governments construct vast stone monuments to celebrate their victories, or large buildings decorated with images of heroic deeds. Their solidity is meant also to suggest the permanence of the government that erected them. Those with few resources can build more fleeting monuments, such as a field of wooden headstones or a fence of yellow ribbons, to send an alternative message about a war and its casualties. Because of the inequality of resources, the stone symbols last longer, but there is no sure method for controlling the interpretations that future generations will apply to the grand monuments they see around them. Today's message of eternal grandeur may be tomorrow's emblem of authoritarian brutality.

We also see the role of **historical narratives**, sometimes called metanarratives, when we look at collective memory. We may see history as a break with the past, in nations founded through a revolution. Or we may see it as a story of continual progress, with economic growth, the expansion of freedom and inclusion, and national pride all supporting each other. (This is often called the Whig view of history, after the eighteenth- and nineteenth-century political parties in the UK and US that were more modernizing and progressive than their rivals.) Or we may cast history more critically as a long decline, usually starting from some key event or process, such as industrialization or immigration. A nostalgia for the past, before the fall, implies a critique of the present. (Remember: just because social movements use history as sources of meaning, this does not mean that historical theories of protest are valid, since this kind of theory instead substitutes its *own* meaning of history for the meanings held by protestors.)

Whether as part of historical narratives or independently of them, *events* are, like individuals, good to think and feel with. We attribute meanings to them, whether by interpreting the intentions of those involved in the event or by seeing the event as leading to some later state of affairs. We perceive characters who played important roles, especially the heroes of myths but also the villains they vanquished. Events can inspire us to imitate them or they can shock us by focusing our anxieties and changing the way we view things. Complex events like a revolution (actually a long series of events that we link together into a story) offer enormous room for interpretation and projection. We attach facts, characters, frames, and moral judgments to them. They also offer occasions for collective gatherings, or celebrations.

Interactions

Books contain words, murals have colors and lines, and monuments have shapes and carvings – all of which can be used as the raw materials for human meanings. But it is only through the actions of people that these materials are transformed into feelings and understandings about the world. People come together with these objects to interact with each other for a variety of purposes. The potential meanings come alive through these engagements. Demonstrations are the obvious interactions (Fillieule and Tartakowsky 2013). But they are often composed of speech acts and elements of ritual.

Rituals make certain key meanings salient for participants. These range from highly formalized rites like those of a religious service, familiar to all participants and designed to express the fundamental beliefs of adherents, to less formal gatherings such as meetings, where those gathered have some sense of shared purpose but lack strict rules about how to proceed or what choices to make. All human interactions have some ritual aspects, in that we have expectations about how to behave – and not behave – and what the other people are like. Rituals are designed to elicit emotions, such as awe, joy, or solidarity, but they can also fail, leaving us bored, sad, and lonely. Face-to-face interactions that make us feel good or bad lead us to seek out or to avoid the same people or situations in the future (Collins 2001, 2004).

Meaning

Old rituals, especially venerable religious rituals, can be adapted for new purposes. Marriage is a good example. Once castigated by feminists as oppressive to women and celebrated by the religious right as the embodiment of family values, weddings are traditional rituals, usually religious, that gay and lesbian activists were able to transform into radical acts of protest in the late 1990s (Taylor et al. 2009). By demanding the same rights and rituals, these activists could insist on marriage as a relationship between two loving people rather than as machinery for procreation. Weddings also allowed lesbians and gays to do character promotion, as the media were filled with stories of couples who had been together for decades, had raised children, were utterly "normal." If they could get married, then they were moral, responsible people. The rituals defined their character.

Speech acts, according to philosophers, are the things we try to accomplish with language (Klimova 2009). These include more than simply *asserting* facts about the world, but also asking or *commanding* another person to do something, *promising* that we will do something, *expressing* our feelings, *naming* something, and *bringing about* a state of affairs ("this meeting is adjourned"). Activists use all these kinds of speech acts in going about their work. The point is that we do things with words; words are not merely meanings in a dictionary but, when put together into utterances, they are forms of action. In order to understand protest movements, we need to grasp what speakers are trying to do, with what intentions, to what audiences. And we need to remember that speech acts are not accomplished only through words, but with additional gestures, a smile, a wink, or a wave.

Free spaces offer potential protestors a place to invent names, debate tactics, and formulate their discomfort without immediate resistance or repression (Evans and Boyte 1986). These are community centers, schools, churches, or even neighborhood bars where like-minded people can joke, gripe, tell stories, and articulate their grievances. Prisons can serve the same function, as repressive regimes sequester their most radical critics together for long periods of time with little to do but share ideas. The women's movement spread in the late 1960s through small consciousness-raising groups in which women shared their complaints without men around to mock or dismiss them. Free spaces can also be intentional incubators for protest, such as workshops in which activists from different groups share their experiences of what tactics have worked. NOW holds a national conference for this purpose. Free spaces are sometimes a solution to the Janus dilemma: by a strong internal focus, they attempt to generate slogans, analyses, and tactics that will be effective when protestors later confront the outside world. (Other times, they encourage a group's isolation.)

The settings in which artful meanings are created and consumed matters. Thus feminists established the National Women's Music Festival precisely to take advantage of the power of music (Staggenborg et al. 1993). What better ritual, itself a kind of pilgrimage, than one carefully constructed for political purposes?

Our bodies, our selves

A small feminist collective first published *Our Bodies, Ourselves* in 1970, and it has been revised and reissued numerous times since, influencing generation after generation of feminist activists and spreading feminist ideas around the world (Davis 2007). Another book that resulted from a movement but also contributed to it, *Our Bodies, Ourselves* appealed to a category of humans who had always been defined in terms of their bodies. A compendium of information about women's health, the book invites each reader to examine, observe, and feel her own body, her own appearance, even when her own impressions conflict with accepted medical dogma. All people live and act through their bodies, to which we attach meanings. We understand others by how they look, whether rejecting them because they do not look like us, or being attracted to them for their beauty.

It is also through our bodies that we experience feelings about the world. We gather information about the physical and social world around us through hundreds of tiny processes, including all our senses, the production of chemicals (some of which, like adrenaline, charge us up, while others calm us down), muscle contractions, and more. Our bodies constantly conduct information that our brains try to put together into a picture of what is happening and how we should react, and most of this activity occurs unconsciously without our realizing it. But it is misleading to think of our brains as somehow separate from the rest of our body: the components of our central nervous system all act together; that's why it's a system. Some of these feeling-thinking processes are visible to those around us, especially a handful of emotions that have distinct facial expressions. So we communicate some of our emotional states whether we intend to or not.

Other bodily displays are quite intentional. We send statements through our clothes, ranging from certain colors that represent a political party or an alliance (green or rainbow, for instance), to accessories such as buttons or t-shirts with slogans or images on them, to tattoos that often express solidarities with others, all the way to styles that do no more than say, "I am the kind of person who defies convention by wearing safety pins in my ear." Sociologists often see the *resistance* of subcultures in unusual choices like these, a rejection of consumer society or at least of one's parents' sensibilities (Hebdige 1979). They are not always overtly political, but these expressions capture a sensibility of refusal out of which protest easily emerges. Our bodies are physical carriers of meaning every bit as important as books, songs, or blogs.

We carry out our intentions through our bodies: how could we not? Like external tools, our bodies can also fail us. We are too frail to face winter weather for the sake of a rally; we leave a march because we are hungry or thirsty. Or we need to urinate, or poop. In other cases, the immediate pleasures of a drink or a joint or a seductive companion win out over the long-run satisfaction of doing the right thing. Lust and love are more than simple bodily urges, of course, but they can draw people away from collective projects. Movement organizers work hard to protect against all these defections, from providing toilets and water at events to – in more authoritarian settings such as revolutionary armies – imposing rules on romantic entanglements (Goodwin 1997).

Table 4 Five types of feelings

Urges	Urgent bodily needs that crowd out other feelings and attention until they are satisfied: lust, hunger, substance addictions, the need to urinate or defecate, exhaustion or pain
Reflex emotions	Fairly quick, automatic responses to events and information, often taken as the paradigm for all emotions: anger, fear, joy, surprise, shock, and disgust
Moods	Energizing or de-energizing feelings that persist across settings and do not normally take direct objects; they can be changed by reflex emotions, as during interactions
Affective commitments or loyalties	Relatively stable feelings, positive or negative, about others or about objects, such as love and hate, liking and disliking, trust or mistrust, respect or contempt
Moral emotions	Feelings of approval or disapproval (including of our own selves and actions) based on moral intuitions or principles, such as shame, guilt, pride, indignation, outrage, and compassion

Feeling-thinking

An emotion is really a verbal label that we apply to a familiar bundle of feelings. For example if I have a surge of adrenaline, increased heartbeat, and a facial expression that bares my teeth and knits my brows, I may say I am angry. (People watching me may realize I am angry before I do.) There are dozens of underlying processes that go into our feelings, especially changes in our biochemistry and muscle contractions, all of which process information about what is going on around us, especially whether things are going well or badly. We are not even aware of most of these feelings, and do not label them as emotions, but they are still helping us cope with the world. They are the raw materials for emotions. I call them **feeling-thinking processes**.

There are several kinds of feeling bundles – emotions – that we need to distinguish (see table 4). Two types are of relatively short duration. *Urges* are signals from our own bodies, such as hunger, fatigue, lust, or the cravings of addiction. They may arise slowly, but they subside as soon as they are satisfied. They are strong feelings, but we don't usually label them emotions (although some other cultures do).

Reflex emotions arise quickly in response to things that happen around us, including new information. These include anger, the emotion that is most often taken to represent the way that emotions operate in politics, with the result that emotions appear disruptive; by overemphasizing anger, scholars have spread the impression that emotions are always a problem, never a solution. Other reflex emotions are fear, surprise, sudden joy or disappointment, and disgust, all of which have distinct bundles of feelings (bodily processes) associated with them. Each has a distinguishing facial expression, allowing us to communicate them easily to others.

Moods normally last longer than urges or reflex emotions; we can carry a mood with us for hours, days, or even longer. A spirited rally leaves us in a good mood, ready to redouble our efforts on behalf of the cause. Bad moods such as resignation or sadness, or at the extreme depression, deflate us, sometimes to the point that we cannot continue. That is the main impact of moods: they affect our level of energy and so our level of activity. The joyous atmosphere at Zuccotti Park or at women's music festivals operates as a mechanism for generating an engaging mood of excitement, anticipation, and a feeling of changing the world.

There are also two types of emotions that are pretty much permanent parts of our lives. We have *affective loyalties* toward individuals, groups, places, and ideas. These basic orientations toward the world include love, respect, and trust – as well as their negative counterparts like hate or mistrust. Collective identities matter because of the feelings we have toward the group. The women's movement flourished through women who felt a solidarity with each other, and faltered when that solidarity broke up along fault lines of class, race, and sexual orientation.

There are also *moral emotions*, whether approval or disapproval like shame and pride, or compassion for other beings. We have moral emotions about our *own* actions (such as shame) as well as about *other people's* actions (such as outrage). Moral emotions are the heart of a social movement, as they provide the way to make claims on others, to enlist them in your vision of the world and to motivate them to participate with enthusiasm. The women's movement was built on indignation, as most protest is.

The affective and the moral commitments provide something like our basic goals in life: whom do we want to help, whom do we trust, what are we ashamed or proud of? We develop both types early in life and tend to stick with them, although affective loyalties can sometimes change, often suddenly as when we feel betrayed. Love can turn to hate. Lesbians felt betrayed by their straight sisters.

Although emotions operate through our bodies (just as our most abstract thoughts are lodged in our brain circuitry), they are heavily influenced by culture. What *triggers* them differs across cultures: different groups are disgusted or angered by different things, even if the resulting facial expressions look similar. And how we *display* our feelings is shaped by culture: men are expected to express anger more than women are; in Japan all overt expressions of anger are discouraged. In addition to triggers and displays, our *labels* for emotional bundles are also cultural: shame has different borders, for example, shading into guilt or embarrassment more quickly in some cultures than in others. An especially big difference in moral emotions is between cultures that attribute more credit and blame to autonomous individuals and those cultures which think more in group terms, such as family honor.

* * *

We have seen all sorts of cultural meanings in this chapter, looking at their physical embodiments and their figurative ones, their appearance in interactions and in our bodies. We examined characters and collective memory. Humans cannot help trying to find meaning in the world, and imposing it on everything they see around them. This is an active process, as they go out and engage the world. They do not simply sit back and watch it. We have seen the role of emotions in these processes of meaning-making. Emotions guide our engagement, as they show us what we care about, what we are attracted to, what repelled by. They help us find our way through complex environments.

But humans have always invented meanings; they have not always developed social movements. Why have protest movements flourished in the modern world, and especially in the last several decades? We turn now to the kind of infrastructures and contexts that help or hinder social movements, but we should not forget that all these capacities help to transmit or block the kinds of cultural meanings we have examined here in chapter 2.

3

Infrastructure

Jesus was no sissy: the Christian Right

The American women's movement of the 1960s, along with other (real and perceived) attacks on traditional culture and institutions, aroused backlash movements among religious conservatives who believed that the Christian Bible contains the literal word of God. And God's intent, according to these groups, is for men to rule over women as God rules over His church, implying different "natural" roles for males and females. Pornography threatened to change the nature of sex, sex education to undermine paternal power over it, and – worst of all – abortion would give women the capacity to plan and control their own childbearing rather than leaving it up to their husbands, and to God's schedule.

The new religious right that entered US politics in the 1970s drew some of its members from earlier conservative movements, especially the anticommunism of the 1950s, which dissolved only with Lyndon Johnson's landslide victory over conservative Barry Goldwater in the 1964 presidential election. In study groups of the John Birch Society, individual activists had learned that America was being threatened by a worldwide conspiracy of communists and socialists, centered on the United Nations. In the late 1960s, bra-less women and long-haired hippies displaced communists as the primary threat to the American way of life, which came to center more on family values than on individual liberties.

Even more directly, the new movement grew out of networks of evangelical and fundamentalist churches, especially throughout the southern and western states. Almost all these churches had avoided politics until the dramatic changes of the late 1960s, and the even more dramatic media depictions of those changes, which made them feel acutely threatened and shocked. The Republican Party, as part of its effort to attract white southerners opposed to black civil rights, recruited these preachers and their flocks (just as the civil rights movement had mobilized black churches a decade earlier). In a distinctive, but not unprecedented, reading of scripture, Jerry Falwell could proclaim that he was a warrior for God. "Jesus was not a pacifist. He was not a sissy."

Two **moral shocks** (events or information so upsetting that people can be recruited more easily) boosted the new movement: Congress's passage of the Equal Rights Amendment in 1972 and the Supreme Court's *Roe v. Wade* decision legalizing abortion in 1973. Feminists were described as witches who had launched a Satanic attack on the American family, so that the movement began to proclaim itself "pro-family" and "pro-life," positive terms that sounded better than "anti-abortion." The initial mobilization against *Roe v. Wade* was spearheaded by the Catholic Church, obviously well organized already, but in the 1980s Protestant fundamentalists took the lead, culminating in the pugnacious activities of Operation Rescue in the late 1980s. This group, dominated by young men angry about women's rights, were indeed warriors, using physical coercion to shut down abortion clinics, screaming, pushing, spitting, and cursing at terrified young women. And at the fringe of the fringe, men burned and blew up clinics and kidnapped, shot, and sometimes killed clinic doctors and other staff.

If the Christian Right felt threatened by the liberal counterculture, it also had a wing that depended on that new culture. Both sides claimed to offer a deeper, more meaningful existence than the crass materialism of shopping malls and mass culture. The Jesus movement in the late 1960s explicitly recruited hippies in southern California, and then elsewhere, combining communal houses, folk music, emotional services, and fundamentalist theology. The right also claimed the label "radical," insisting that they were not conserving the status quo but trying to change American society in fundamental ways. Like women and African Americans, conservative activists felt excluded and disrespected, as if the main institutions of their country had been taken over by educated elites and liberal intellectuals who treated them with contempt.

Broad movements like the religious right or the women's movement, composed of hundreds or thousands of small groups and individual adherents, do not appear from nowhere, nor do they usually disappear completely. Both individuals and the cultural meanings that inspire them are around for future mobilization, when old ideas take on new forms and new villains. They borrow and transform existing **infrastructure**, which includes communications, transportation, financial and legal systems, meeting rooms, social networks, formal organizations, and all the other capacities that allow people to get things done. Protestors use infrastructure to promulgate their cultural meanings.

The Christian Right shows that religion and social movements interact in several ways. Foremost, religions begin and spread as movements, through some of the same processes of recruitment and motivation as other movements (although forcible conversion is more common in religious movements, once they come to control states and armies). These are religious movements in the narrowest sense. In a second pattern, religion offers cultural meanings, free spaces, and other infrastructure to other movements, as in the example I am here describing as the Christian Right in the US. A third possibility is that movements within religions try to change them, as Liberation Theology attempted to alter the Catholic Church in the 1970s. Faith in God, an afterlife, good and evil, and other fundamental beliefs about the world can provide powerful motivations for action. What better spur to action than a fear of rotting in hell if you do not stand up against sin?

We also see here how opposed movements inspire each other, with each success by one side becoming a threat that mobilizes the other. Gains by women in the 1960s then by gays and lesbians in the 1970s were moral shocks for rightwing Christians, whose homophobia in turn inspired more militant organizing in the LGBTQ community (lesbian, gay, bisexual, transsexual, and queer), and so on. If one side enters an arena, the other side follows it (Fetner 2008).

Most scholars of social movements are left-leaning in their own politics, and most study movements they admire. The result has been that, despite all the sophistication of theories of protest, scholars often use different kinds of theories to explain movements of the left and of the right. Accounts of left-liberal movements are sympathetic, looking at the nuances of difficult decisions, accepting movement goals as reasonable, taking insider accounts at face value. Accounts of the right tend to be more psychological, devoting attention to cognitive and emotional pathologies that could mislead protestors, looking for secret funding by corporations or political parties, and downplaying protestors' own reasons for their action. Participant observation and introspection (reflecting on one's own experiences) are common methods for studying left-liberal movements but absent from research on rightwing movements.

We may need to apply more psychology to the left, but we certainly need to apply less pejorative models to the right. We need to apply what I call the *normal-person test* to our theories: would we use the same kinds of factors to explain our own actions? Do we portray those we study as normal people, capable of mistakes but acting on the basis of their own vision of the world, trying to advance their various moral projects? Or do we present them as so misguided, disturbed, and relentless that they seem abnormal?

Protest movements always maneuver through layers of cultural and political context, taking advantage of any opportunities they find. New sources of income, sudden weaknesses in opponents, new arenas, shifts in broad understandings are all openings for activists, if they are savvy and nimble enough to recognize and take advantage of them. Those who lack resources can often compensate with intelligent strategic choices. But there are some basic preconditions to the emergence of a movement, even to movements generally. We began to look at these in chapter 1, but we now need to elaborate on other advantages that a movement

Research techniques

Scholars have used all sorts of research methods to understand protest, some of which are especially sensitive to cultural meanings and some of which are not. Structural and historical theories tend to rely on quantitative data about events, counting how many riots, marches, petitions, and so on there were in each month or year over long periods. These can be correlated with other big changes, such as the growing importance of parliament or changes in economic conditions. These *event histories* are mostly drawn from newspaper accounts and police records. They cannot usually get at what the events mean to the people participating, although they sometimes show what the events mean to police and journalists.

To get at participants' understandings and feelings, culturally oriented scholars have looked at protestors' own writings and speeches, often teasing out the rhetorical techniques or the stories used. More often, researchers look at movements of their own day, so that they can use *participant observation* and *interviews* to understand what protestors are thinking and feeling. If they participate themselves, they can use *introspection* to assess their own reactions, calculations, and emotions in order to guess what others are going through, and they can confirm or falsify these hunches through interviews. *Experiments* can show how people think, make decisions, and feel emotions – raw materials for political action. Finally, most scholars of movements use *case studies*, so that they can look at one movement in depth, a technique which also has its drawbacks: they don't know if their theory applies to other movements, and they tend to become cheerleaders for that movement, unable to see its flaws as well as its strengths. This kind of *engaged research* is part advocacy and part explanation.

relies on, especially political arenas open to citizens, media outlets, social networks, and formal organizations. In the background of all these are capitalist markets, which affect the distribution of resources in every society.

Citizenship

Political contexts are crucial to most social movements, affecting how they start up and what they do. Some of the largest social movements in history have aimed at expanding citizenship, whether by adding new rights or by bringing new people into the polity. As we saw with "Wilkes and Liberty," new rights to assemble and communicate aid new mobilization, which in turn pushes for new rights. Many of the participants in the Wilkes agitation did not have sufficient property to allow them to vote, but hoped eventually to get the franchise (as their grandchildren ultimately did).

In most countries, the road to full democratic participation has been slow and violent, with many setbacks along the way. Citizenship movements – including early labor movements, women's suffrage, civil rights, and today's immigrant rights efforts – aim at gaining entry into the political system, and they usually advance when they find sympathetic elites already inside. Some members of the new groups even reach the commanding heights of existing institutions: elite positions in politics, business, and universities.

Factions of political insiders open the door to newcomers for a variety of reasons. In some cases, they see new supporters who will help them in their existing battles, much as the Democratic Party in the US expected new black voters to support them – as they have, overwhelmingly, ever since the Civil Rights Act of 1964. In many cases, this is the result of normal electoral calculations. In rare cases, segments of the elite have ideological commitments: for instance, they have made statements in favor of democratic principles, and they can be shamed into following those principles. In a third type of case, probably the most common, elites make concessions because they fear worse consequences if they do not. Mass strikes and riots have frightened many politicians into conciliatory laws. In all cases, politicians seek strategic gains in their own arenas, and new voters or laws may help them in all sorts of ways. Groups remain loyal to the party that gives them the vote.

Political rights are about the persuasive influence of people on the state. Some are about who is part of the polity, others about what they can do there. Are there free and fair elections for both executives and legislators? Are there open electoral laws and campaigns? Are government agencies corrupt or indifferent to the public? Can new parties be created? Is there an opposition and does it have any power?

Civil rights have more to do with the state's coercive interference in the lives of citizens. Does it prevent people from assembling or publishing their views? Does it allow political organizations and trade unions to form? Are the police and military under civilian control? Are people imprisoned, exiled, tortured, or terrorized? Is there freedom of travel, work, and residence? Are property rights secure? Is there sexual freedom and marital choice?

Human or **civil rights movements** are about ending coercion, torture, detention, bodily harm, and so on; citizenship movements aim at expanding the realm of persuasion through new people and new channels of influence. When an oppressed group gains political rights, it usually uses these to gain civil rights as well. Civil rights do not always lead to political rights, however, perhaps because a focus on civil rights characterizes a group as victims without the strength to fight for their own political rights (Seidman 2007). Civil rights are not as empowering as political rights.

The political context is different for a third type of movement, **post-citizenship movements,** composed of those who already have the basic rights of citizens and are demanding other kinds of things, such as protections for the environment, changes in the criminal penalties for drug use or drunk driving, or greater economic equality (Jasper 1997). Because they already have the primary rights of citizens, participants in post-citizenship movements often aim at benefits for others: all of humanity, generations not yet born, those suffering in other countries, even other species. Religious movements are usually post-citizenship movements, except when they are the effort of a religious minority to gain basic rights. (Many religious movements, like the Christian Right in the US, *claim* to be oppressed, since this gains them sympathy and mobilizes members.) In most wealthy countries, movements inspired by religious ideologies tend to aim for moral programs such as a ban on abortion or for the right of women to wear headscarves.

The distinction between citizenship and post-citizenship movements is not always clear, since many movements aim at extending the idea of rights. The right to marry is not usually thought of as a component of citizenship – except to those same-sex couples who are excluded from it, and who realize the many benefits it entails, such as the right to visit one's partner in the hospital. Do citizens have a *right* not to live near a nuclear reactor or a hazardous waste dump? Does a fetus have civil rights, or is it part of its mother's body, subject to her medical choices?

The main contested territory, however, is economic: do people have a *right* to housing, education, healthcare, a job? Do they have a right to inherit the family business? The family fortune? Are citizens' rights undermined by extreme inequality, which imposes shame on those at the bottom and encourages arrogance in those at the top? Many movements try to reframe private hardships as issues of public rights and responsibilities. It took several hundred years for human and political rights to be accepted principles in most of the world, and the process is still not complete. It may take just as long to establish economic rights, especially because powerful players, namely for-profit corporations, are fighting hard against the idea.

The rights of citizens are a crucial infrastructure for protest because they shape the costs of different kinds of actions. Protest is risky where the police abuse human rights, less so where the police are discouraged from mistreating suspects. Political rights are an enormous leap forward for any group, allowing it to participate in new ways. Rights are both a fundamental goal of movements, and the means to attaining many other goals. They are also an inspiring moral vision, having spread around the world to give hope to potential protestors everywhere.

Gaining voice

If protest is channeled by political institutions and infrastructure, it is also affected by the media available for conveying its moral vision, for this determines its audience. History has seen a vast expansion in the possibilities for transmitting people's views, from exclusively face-to-face conversations up through global news media. Activists try to promulgate their ideas as widely as possible, but in most cases the broader the medium the less they can control the messages it conveys. New communications technologies since the nineteenth century have sustained social movements – but also supported efforts to monitor and suppress them. Media are a key physical resource, even if they matter most because of the cultural meanings that are transmitted over them.

We saw that social movements of all sorts appeared in the nineteenth century, in part because the rapid growth of cities made transportation and communications easier. In crammed working-class neighborhoods, the beating of some pots could bring crowds into the street to build a barricade or march on the local police barracks. Trams, subways, and buses would eventually allow hundreds of thousands to flood public places for protest events. Workplaces also grew in size. A strike at one of the giant factories that appeared in the twentieth century could involve thousands rather than the dozens who might be employed at a diminutive rural factory.

Communication also improved, especially with the invention of cheap (and politically engaged) newspapers. Potential insurgents no longer had to go to coffeehouses to follow events, especially as literacy also increased (although coffeehouses – only found in cities – were unusually sheltered, democratic, free spaces where radical ideas could be debated and developed). Political debates allowed large numbers of people to develop ideologies. Casual rumors still played a role in mobilizing people, but the average city-dweller was getting more sophisticated intellectually. As we saw, social movements in the US took a great step forward in the 1830s with the mass printing and mailing of bibles and religious tracts.

The reach of the media has continued to expand, with radio and then television penetrating more and more homes, workplaces, and squares around the world. Later, the internet opened up channels for less centralized, less one-directional messaging (Earl and Kimport 2011). *Social media* such as Facebook and Twitter tap into existing social networks, and so allow communication through them. Protest movements like Moveon.org in the US and "We Are All Khaled Said" in Egypt learned to mobilize large numbers of protestors through email blasts, and to react quickly through mass cellphone messages. Struggles continue over these media, which are not as decentralized as they seem, but depend on large companies that can shut down service or allow government censorship and surreptitious monitoring.

Many protestors are obsessed with media coverage, inventing colorful events to attract attention, whether "levitating" the Pentagon, a 1966 "sip-in" for the right of gay men to be served in bars, or **flash mobs**, a kind of guerrilla theater organized by cellphone blasts, including "carrotmobs" that patronize a store in exchange for its commitment to make desired improvements such as green retrofitting. Some groups pursue coverage to the exclusion of other worthy – and perhaps more effective – goals (Sobieraj 2011). They sometimes forget that the media are not only an arena, but also a set of players with their own goals (see chapter 7). Protestors may attract attention, but they have little control over the nature of that attention: in many cases the protestors and their photogenic actions are the story, while their arguments are ignored.

The media are big business, and even small, autonomous media efforts are eventually absorbed into the mainstream. Those who own the media have most of the biases of others who own corporations; they especially dislike talk about the drawbacks of private ownership (Bagdikian 2004). They are also frequently cozy with top government officials, through social networks as well as through their work. Even reporters come to rely heavily on government sources. When big media are not private companies, they are government agencies, reflecting a different set of biases, namely the ideology of the state, which can be just as antithetical to protest goals.

In response, social movements often create their own media outlets. If it is a small movement, this may be nothing more than an occasional newsletter, but a large movement may have its own

The media dilemma

Protest groups usually wish to reach large numbers of people, whether to get their message out or to recruit members, and established media are an effective way to do this. But the attention they get is not always favorable because it reflects the biases of reporters, editors, and owners. Protestors try to influence the content, through announcements written in advance, the selection and training of spokespersons, and careful stagecrafting of events. But in all strategic engagements, other players (in this case the media) add an element of unpredictability. In the worst case, media attention can arouse a backlash that discredits or destroys the protest movement. The media often view protestors as local color, not spokespeople in serious public controversies: the gimmicks or disruption that gets them in the door prevents them from being taken seriously (Gamson and Wolfsfeld 1993). This is a version of the powerful-allies dilemma confronting all strategic players (more on this in chapter 7): you may need a powerful ally for its resources or connections, but it is just as likely that it will use you for its own ends, as that it will help you attain yours. The media will use you to attract audiences more than they help you get your issue out there.

radio or television station or newspaper. Today, websites, blogs, and listserves are cheap enough for any group. The term "fundamentalism" itself derives from a publishing project launched in 1910 by the Bible Institute of Los Angeles. Twelve volumes of essays – titled *The Fundamentals* – laid out a complete ideology of Protestant fundamentalism, acerbically distinguishing it from Romanism, Mormonism, liberal protestants, Jehovah's Witnesses, and Christian Science, as well as attacking more secular ideologies like liberalism, socialism, and evolution (Marsden 2006). The books were remarkably successful at inspiring the fundamentalist attack on all sorts of twentieth-century developments and ideas, not only through their arguments but also through the social networks they relied upon and reinforced, still available in the 1970s.

Most social movements seize an issue considered a private matter and try to make it a problem of public morality, and media are crucial to this shift. Typically, we first hear about a new issue through a news report about a small protest, which is often treated with amusement or disbelief. Later, we may notice editorials, which still scoff at the protestors but at least take the issue seriously enough to address it. It is now a legitimate public controversy, and may eventually come to be acknowledged as a public problem that needs to be fixed.

New media convey movement messages more easily thanks to the increasing levels of education in most of the world's nations. Cheap newspapers and text messages are more effective when most of the population is literate. Those who have spent years in higher education have greater capacities (and tolerance of obscure writing styles) to develop elaborate ideologies, with supporting arguments and evidence easily at their disposal. Education also provides many of the skills and credentials to run organizations.

Informal networks

Social networks, with which we communicate with others, are the building blocks of human interaction, and nothing happens – including protest – without them. We enlist people we know to attend a rally with us; we get information about events through our friends and family; we share ideas and emotions with those around us. We rarely go to a meeting or a march alone; we go with one or two family or friends.

It is easy to picture networks as a web of physical connections, like circuits in a computer chip or roads on a map. In this structural image, people react automatically when their networks are switched on. A more cultural view of networks is that individuals have patterns of emotional bonds, backed up by cognitive symbols and familiarity. When my sister asks me to drive her to Earth Day in Albany, I am more likely to say yes than if I receive an email from a stranger or an organization. I have known my sister all my life, enjoy spending time with her, and trust her political loyalties.

I feel positively toward those in my social networks, mostly. Another cultural way to think about networks is that they provide opportunities for us to persuade others, sometimes transforming the networks in the process (Mische 2003).

Some networks already exist, and an emerging movement tries to tap into them. For older members of the Christian Right, the John Birch Society had played the role of a "boot camp" for activists, who formed lasting bonds as well as developing an ideology that could be adapted to new causes (McGirr 2001: 223). Protestant congregations could be recruited to the emerging movement through their preachers. In other cases a movement tries to nurture its own networks of people who care about an issue. Whether old or new, the networks are infrastructure that enable protest groups to spread information and mobilize participants. They keep people coming back, to enjoy old friends, to feel like a good person, to catch up on the latest news.

Informal networks can grow into **subcultures**, with distinctive styles of dress, tastes in tactics, and ideas not shared by the rest of society. Subcultures form a kind of hothouse where new moral intuitions can be encouraged and lived out, and where ideas can be expressed without inspiring repression or facing ridicule. This is especially likely when they have their own free spaces that help build networks through face-to-face interactions.

Networks and organizations reinforce each other. American fundamentalists, over the course of the twentieth century, began with their own churches and a publishing house, but eventually developed a network of schools all the way from nurseries through PhD programs, their own think-tanks and theological seminaries, and all the institutions necessary for a distinctive culture. Although these are supposed to be sheltered spaces free of government surveillance, preachers and others in these networks often say extreme things that the mainstream media pick up: Jews and Catholics will go to hell, the nation's ills are due to its tolerance for gays and lesbians, and so on. Free spaces try to avoid the audience-segregation dilemma through privacy (see chapter 7), but they do not always succeed.

These networks and organizations occasionally give birth to

more visible protest in public arenas, especially when a decision or event attracts attention and stokes indignation. This is one reason that large protests can appear so rapidly: there is already an infrastructure to help mobilize people. This consists not just of a phone tree or email list (or Christmas-card list, for Christian activists), but also of patterns of trust, respect, and fondness that draw people at an emotional level. They can nurture each other's outrage, hate, compassion, and other feelings that will, eventually, support public protest.

The Janus dilemma appears in the contrast between the private, hidden nature of subcultural networks and the public nature of protest intended to reach broader publics. Active protest may demand more from people than they are comfortable with, or it may inspire a public backlash that challenges the protected lifestyle of those networks. Many social movements encourage private activities as part of their efforts at social change: recycling, responsible consumption, planting trees, reading the Bible, avoiding birth control. That is why social movements and protest movements, although they overlap, are not entirely the same, and their activities are sometimes in conflict. You can accomplish a lot as a social movement without public protest.

Formal organizations

In order to sustain their efforts, protestors create formal organizations, complete with stationery, a website, regular officers and staffs, and other signs that they should be taken seriously. The modern era has invented and extended many bureaucratic mechanisms to create and sustain organizations: organizational charts, rules, hiring and firing procedures, filing cabinets and other office equipment, time schedules, management techniques, record-keeping, and so on. The advantages of having organizations are obvious: they can hire staff; they can rent a place to meet, make phone calls, keep a computer; they can establish rules and routines so that there is no need to discuss everything every day; they can seek donations of time and money that will keep the cause alive

The organization dilemma

Protestors face many choices about how much to formalize their operations through rules, fundraising, paid staff, and offices. Formalities like these help sustain activities over time, but they can also change those activities. The goal of sustaining and protecting the organization appears alongside its original mission, and more time is devoted to raising funds and expanding staffs. In some cases, the survival of the organization becomes the primary goal. Members may then grow cynical about staff salaries, the paid trips leaders take on official business, large and lavish offices. Laws governing the operation of officially incorporated organizations – especially their tax-exempt status – constrain their tactical choices. Organizations are like other strategic means: they always have the potential to become ends in themselves, a case of the sorcerer's-apprentice dilemma that we saw earlier.

even as individuals come and go. Formal organizations are the heart of many movements, and yet, as the organization dilemma summarizes, they pose costs and risks as well.

One of the advantages of formal organizations is that they can be used to systematically raise funds for a social movement: they apply for foundation grants; they buy email lists (formerly they bought mailing addresses); and they cultivate wealthy individuals sympathetic to the cause – just as all nonprofits do. Activists approach wealthy individuals through personal networks, but the more anonymous email blasts – to the members of an organization or subscribers to a magazine – are a kind of pre-existing network as well. Protest organizations aim to attract money from both individuals and foundations. To the extent that an organization grows, it relies more on money.

Organizations also help to establish familiar routines of protest that make it easier to pull off events. People with the right know-how are either active in a movement or can be hired as consultants. Most of the time, organizations prefer legal tactics to illegal ones, since the latter can lead the police to arrest their leaders and shut down the organization. The organization itself becomes a potential hostage in interactions with authorities.

Viewed from the outside, organizations look like players, with shared visions, goals, and tactical tastes. Scholars certainly treat them that way, based on their official statements, brochures, and the actions they sponsor. But when you look inside an organization, it is also an arena, in which various individuals and factions disagree, threaten each other, and battle over every decision. We will see in chapter 6 that these battles unfold in different ways, but we should never forget them, we should never pretend that a complex group is ever a completely unified group.

Professionals

Not everyone in an organization has the same skills or influence. As movement organizations grow larger, they often rely on **professional staff** rather than on volunteers: people who are paid to be there rather than (or in addition to) working out of enthusiasm for the cause. Organizations can control staff more easily than volunteers, who are also often more radical in their goals than staff are. On the other hand, in a society where there are hundreds or thousands of movement organizations, there is room for professional militants who have a lifetime of experience doing politics, making decisions, reacting quickly to windows of opportunity, and generally honing their instincts about good and bad choices. They avoid many mistakes. Full-time activists are usually involved in several causes at the same time: one where they are paid, another where they live, still others where they volunteer. To sustain extensive participation without burning out, they must weave activism into their everyday lives, and the best way to do this is to be paid for being an activist.

This idea of an **activist career** suggests that individuals operate through organizations, but sometimes also outside of them (Fillieule 2010). They move in and out of groups and of organizations over time, and they take skill and know-how with them as they do. A career has its own logic, of commitment and of development, independent of the logic of organizations. Different forms of participation are open to individuals at different times in their lives, and their experiences in each phase affect the options they have in future phases through the skills, contacts, and identities they develop. These patterns help explain why women and men often end up in different roles in movements, especially when men tend to get the paid positions and women the unpaid tasks. The idea of activist careers reminds us of the importance of education as an external infrastructure to which protest movements can turn.

Moral entrepreneurs, we saw, invent new frames and causes that they hope will attract attention and sympathy, and lead to the mobilization of a new group or movement. Indignation might be widespread, but it requires someone to name it, offer a path of action, and do the initial work of calling people together. The term "entrepreneur" has unsavory implications of self-interest, but these people do a great deal of cultural work in persuading others of a new cause. They invent and adapt images, characters, stories, and other cultural meanings, hoping to find those that resonate with potential participants. Someone had to figure out, through trial and error, that the term "unborn baby," combined with sonograms of fetuses and lapel pins of tiny feet, would mobilize more people than formal Latin edicts from the Catholic Church. "Babies" arouse stronger emotions than "embryos" or "fetuses" or lengthy documents titled "Evangelium Vitae."

The extensive infrastructure of protest in modern societies – the organizations, laws governing them, fundraising experts and companies, vast know-how spread through extensive informal networks of seasoned activists, and so on – has led scholars to speak of a **social movement society** in which protest has become a regular part of politics (Meyer and Tarrow 1997). Because it is easier to do, it has lost its power to intimidate authorities, attract media attention, or even to prove the strength of protestors' moral and emotional commitments. Audiences for protest do a little mental arithmetic: do 100,000 signatures on an online petition equal 1,000 humans standing outside on a cold winter day? But even if protest tends to be routinized over time, protestors always have the capacity to break out of those routines by making different tactical choices: suddenly a Tea Partier begins disrupting town hall meetings, a multitude occupies Zuccotti Park, or the Mubarak regime is driven from office. Protest no longer seems so tame, or so normal.

Capitalism

Patterns of production and income distribution are always an influential context for protest as both a source of grievances and part of the infrastructure. Slaves face tighter surveillance than peasants, factory workers than doctors. Every system of control is a potential source of grievance. Struggles occur in the workplace not just over how much money people will be paid, but also over how many hours they work, when they work them, how intensively they work during those hours, and (this is a big one) how they are treated by their bosses. A lot of strikes and other resistance are triggered when employees feel they have not been respected, not given the dignity that all humans deserve. In many cases, the spark is one foreman saying something inappropriate to one employee.

Just as importantly, the economy determines who has how much money to spend on protest or on blocking protest. McCarthy and Zald (1977) were impressed that a new middle class had discretionary income to contribute to their favorite causes, increasing the total amount of protest in contemporary societies.

But the rich have the most money. Encouraged by the resurgent right in the 1980s, Margaret Thatcher in the UK and Ronald Reagan in the US led a backlash, funded by corporations and the wealthy, against the welfare state's efforts to equalize incomes and protect the vulnerable. Rich people learned how to use their resources to influence politicians, at first Tories and Republicans but eventually Labour and Democrats too. Money changed everything. To take one example that demonstrates how much the political spectrum shifted, Republican president Richard Nixon created the Environmental Protection Agency in 1970, considered a negative income tax to help the poor, and at least claimed to support affirmative action – progressive measures that Democrat president Bill Clinton did not support a quarter century later, after the great backlash had pushed both US parties to the right.

Corporations and wealthy families work hard at keeping their money, and at getting more. This does not mean they deserve it, since one of the ways they work hardest is not at making useful products but at influencing government policies and politicians in blatantly corrupt ways. They hire financial advisors to help them avoid taxes, lobbyists to promote their interests. They contribute vast sums to political candidates, to whom they have unusual access when they need it. The financial industry goes wild when any bill is proposed that would redistribute income, and politicians almost always back down. Remarkably, conservative ideologues in the US have made "free markets" seem like a Christian issue.

In addition to the ways that the economy distributes the means to influence political decisions, the distribution of income and wealth is a potential grievance in and of itself; in fact it was *the* central motivation and target for Occupy and related movements. Although resentment of the rich is always there, it takes cultural work for it to mobilize people. An *unequal* income distribution has to be interpreted as *unjust*, and markets must be seen as capable of human intervention, otherwise people fatalistically accept the state of things. (We'll talk more about blame later.)

Markets generate inequality, but governments can alleviate those inequalities if they wish. On the positive side, markets are efficient ways to distribute goods and services and information without central planning. This is why repressive regimes always try to control them. Money brings freedom, especially compared to coercion, but also compared to the long interactions that persuasion requires. The most repressive regimes are those that control the economy as well as the polity. And the power of money is why inequality undermines democracy.

Globalization

Before the nineteenth century almost all protest was local, concentrating on the neighborhood baker who was charging too much for bread, or the local lord who was requiring too much work from his peasants. In the late eighteenth century and especially the nineteenth century, as the necessary infrastructures spread, protest became national, aimed at parliaments as the key arenas. In recent decades, networks of communications, transportation, money, and organizations have continued to extend their reach, linking people in different countries more easily than ever before, in a process known as **globalization.**

Protestors in one location can follow events elsewhere, learn new tactics, and inspire each other instantly, without being in the same place. But if they do wish to visit each other, transportation has also become faster and cheaper. Global infrastructures have expanded, whether or not some of the more extreme claims are also true (that there is a single emerging global culture or global market, or that nation-states are becoming obsolete).

Just as protest movements once prided themselves on being national rather than local efforts, today they aim to be worldwide, as with the global justice movement (see chapter 6). One of the first movements to rely on global networks, in fact the movement that helped develop them, was the movement against South African apartheid. This effort, present from the beginning of apartheid in 1948, got international recognition after police killed 69 people in Sharpeville in 1960. The media attention was supplemented and sustained by a worldwide network of activists who had been exiled by the apartheid government, living especially in many of the world's media centers and political capitals (Thörn 2006).

As soon as we recognize the global reach of protest we can see that national states are not the only arena where decisions are made. The United Nations and the European Union contain multiple arenas where laws and guidelines are developed, even if these are still largely enforced by national governments. A global perspective encourages us to be more precise about the arenas and players we are discussing. And once we set aside the idea that a state is a unified player, we can see all the diverse arenas inside its borders as well as those outside it.

In recent years religious conservatives have followed other protest groups into the new, international arenas that have proliferated. Some of these campaigns are simply interventions into existing national arenas, as when the US-based Alliance Defense Fund filed a brief in Romanian courts in support of a (successful) suit to define marriage as a bond between a man and a woman rather than two "spouses."

Other arenas are explicitly global, most obviously the United Nations and its various units, where the Vatican has used its "special observer" status to support the global "Baptist-burqa" network of fundamentalist religious organizations. Religious groups have learned to use the human rights talk at the core of the UN's mission, rejecting any criticism of their illiberal positions as itself "violations of fundamental human rights," namely the right to religious beliefs (Bob 2012: 51). As in Romania, religious groups have undermined or at least blocked the advance of gay rights in many parts of the world. The resources and legitimacy that western organizations bring to poor nations can have big payoffs.

Despite these international arenas, most global activism is still focused on the agencies of national states. Capitalism remains more global than protest against it, even though the global justice movement tried to change that. For most anti-capitalist protestors, a global justice movement is still an aspiration, a rallying cry, a process, rather than a finished product. But the battleground is more and more global: for every Disney movie exported from Hollywood, there is a critique that circulates; for every t-shirt shipped from Bangladesh to London, there is a watchdog group trying to check on sweatshop conditions. If there is a global commodity culture, there is also a global human rights and justice culture (Silver 2003). The same kinds of infrastructure that ship the t-shirts open the way for social movements.

* * *

We have seen three ways to get what you want as a political or strategic player: through physical coercion or the threat of it; by paying others to do things they might not otherwise do; and by persuading people to embrace your goals and take the time to pursue them. We have now seen that broad political, economic, organizational, and technological institutions and infrastructure affect all of these. We can also now see a fourth way to get what you want: you can have members of your team in positions in hierarchies where they control coercion, payments, and the means of persuasion. The more organizations there are, the more such positions there are. Modern societies are filled with formal organizations; they are the way we get things done including protest.

Money, organizations, networks, political institutions, and media: the distribution of these is more or less fixed for a social movement when it starts off. They are all structural mechanisms, we might say. But the movement tries hard to change all of them: to raise money, build new networks and organizations, make political allies, attract media attention, even intervene in markets. Protestors do all these things – and their opponents try to block them – through the meanings they create and convey. Culture animates the infrastructures, just as the latter help spread culture. We turn now to the many ways that protestors try to have these effects, beginning with how they recruit new members to the cause.

4

Recruiting

Get used to it: LGBTQ movements

To put things simply, in the early twentieth century physicians, social workers, and other high-minded professionals invented homosexuality. Men had had sex with men, and women with women, throughout human history, but "homosexuality" was an all-encompassing identity that defined them as a certain kind of person through and through. It was about who they were, their desires, not about what they actually did. There had often been a stigma surrounding sex between men in the past (no one cared much about what women did), but only for the bottoms, not the tops. For thousands of years, even in places like ultra-macho Rome, masculinity had meant sticking your dick wherever you wanted. With the new diagnosis came mid-century efforts to cure, control, and exclude gays and lesbians from polite places (Chauncey 1994; Katz 1995).

So they found their own places to get together, in some cases, not only bars and nightclubs but entire neighborhoods like Greenwich Village in New York or Motzstrasse in Berlin. They also established their own organizations, such as the Mattachine Society (founded 1950) and the Daughters of Bilitis (1955), which functioned as social clubs sheltered from the police raids that public bars endured. With the purpose of these organizations kept obscure to outsiders, they could only recruit people through personal contacts and so remained tiny. (This is hardly the only movement that has used lust, in part, to recruit new members.)

In June 1969, in response to yet another police raid on a Greenwich Village bar, patrons and passers-by gathered outside the Stonewall Inn. Rough police treatment increased their anger, and they began throwing coins, apparently because of a rumor that the mafia-owned bar had been raided for failing to pay off the police. Pennies turned to bottles, bricks, high heels, and garbage cans, and a battle followed between police and a chorus line of drag queens (among others). The riots continued off and on for several days. The hidden gay community swelled with pride as well as anger.

Gay pride parades, days, and weekends, at first intended to commemorate Stonewall each year, gave focus to a new gay liberation movement, drawing on the rights language honed by African Americans, women, American Indians, and others in the 1960s. Groups formed on college campuses, thousands flocked to gay enclaves in most of the world's great cities, bathhouses and discos encouraged sexual freedom, and the excited mood of liberation was everywhere.

Homophobic counterattacks in the 1970s, by the growing Christian Right, only strengthened lesbian and gay identities and communities, while also giving them a political edge. Just to be gay or lesbian felt political, as if the entire community were mobilized. "Coming out" was both a personal and a political act, almost a duty to one's comrades. It also made one's life easier, eventually.

This heady excitement lasted a decade, until the AIDS epidemic emerged at the beginning of the 1980s, forcing most members of gay communities to devote their attention to caring for the dying, attending funerals, and protecting their own health. Recently empowered rightwing preachers perceived the epidemic as God's punishment for homosexual sins, and President Ronald Reagan refused to even utter the word AIDS, much less expand funding for research and drug development. Frustration, anger, and indignation mounted, but gay activists still mostly tried to demonstrate their loving, normal side, to prove they were just like straight folks. Most wanted to be "respectable," proving their enormous capacities to care for the dying.

Despite these efforts, the US Supreme Court ruled in the 1986 *Bowers v. Hardwick* case that lesbians and gays were not full citizens with the rights to privacy and sex that other citizens had, or, more technically, that each US state had the right to ban homosexual acts without offering any "compelling interest" other than the state legislature's vague sense that they are wrong. Here was a moral shock that outraged those who were already politically active in the gay community, and which almost overnight drew thousands more into activism (Gould 2009). Younger demonstrators began blocking traffic, occupying offices, and aggressively finding ways to channel their anger, leading within months to the creation of ACT UP and similar groups that declared themselves queer, in contrast to the gay and lesbian groups that had been devoted to respectable politics. "What do we want?" went one chant, "Sodomy! When do we want it? Now!" ACT UP was creative, aggressive, and hip; its meetings replaced funerals as the cool place to cruise for partners.

Most movements first develop from the efforts of a small number of individuals, often participants in related social movements, who pick up on emerging cultural concerns and opportunities. They convince others to join them, either by persuading the leaders of existing groups or by spreading their vision through their own social networks. They try to package their ideas, images, and morals in striking shocks, or to take advantage of shocks created by others, like the Stonewall police raid. Recruitment is usually a long path through a number of small steps, not a sudden conversion – and the same mechanisms that first mobilize people also keep them involved.

Around the kitchen table

The image of moral entrepreneurs that we saw earlier, who figure out what causes they can "sell" to the public, exaggerates the solitary nature of the work that goes into first putting a social movement together. More often, it is a conversation among a handful of activists who have become concerned with a new issue, perhaps sparked by a government action they consider outrageous. Since activists know other activists, this could occur in a living room, or at a meal around a kitchen table, a private form of free space and hence among the most free. It may also occur at a more formal gathering: a panel at a conference, an assembly where a faction decides to concentrate on an emerging new issue. In the weeks and months after Stonewall, the Mattachine Society helped coordinate conversations about how the Village could protect its gay bars from brutal police raids. After the *Hardwick* decision, the gay and lesbian rights movement was partly retooled into the queer liberation movement, a frame or sensibility that appealed especially to younger audiences.

These initial groups are not always activists. A cluster of parents, perhaps acquainted through the Parent Teacher Association, might get together when a school closing is announced. Neighbors might meet when a new facility – a jail, public housing, or shopping mall – is proposed for their street or neighborhood. Many women's consciousness-raising groups were formed around old friendships. The point is that a number of people have similar reactions to the same information and events. What results is the "politics of small things," small things that can grow into big things (Goldfarb 2006).

Occupy Wall Street started with an ad in an anti-capitalist magazine, *Adbusters*, but joined forces with a tiny coalition of leftwing groups calling itself New Yorkers against Budget Cuts, which had sponsored a two-week encampment across the street from City Hall in June 2011, dubbed Bloombergville after the billionaire mayor. Activists talk to one another, and they know what to do when they have a good idea. Facebook pages may also trigger discussions, which in turn are the nucleus for meetings and action.

But the basic insight behind the concept of the moral entrepreneur, that a small group of people must take on a considerable burden in the initial stages, seems right. That burden is smaller if those individuals already have access to sympathetic networks or a protest organization, and if there is some event that they can craft into a moral shock, taking advantage of the attention. These rare individuals must still devote time and energy to causes that may come to nothing. They are even more heroic than most protestors.

Networks and meanings

As we saw in chapter 3, social networks are the paths along which action moves, and they are especially crucial to mobilization. They help a movement emerge in the first place, as recruitment usually occurs through networks that existed for other purposes. The best predictor of who will join a movement is whether they know someone who is already part of the movement (Snow et al. 1980). There is a bit of circularity to this research finding, since it makes it hard to account for movements that are just beginning: there is no one in these movements yet. But it helps make sense of how a fully fledged movement attracts newcomers. In most mature movements, a majority of participants were recruited through personal networks. When you go to a rally or a march, you want to have someone to talk to.

These networks are not simply friends and family; in many cases they are based on membership in formal protest organizations. You sign a petition or contribute to a group like the Human Rights Campaign, America's largest LGBT lobbying group, and almost every day you get emails asking you to sign online petitions, contribute money, or do other small things. Or a union decides to march at an Occupy rally, getting out thousands of members. Or activists we know from past campaigns call and ask us to turn out for a new but related cause. ACT UP grew fast because it could rely on tightly knit communities in big cities, but also on networks that other political efforts had constructed over a decade or longer. The more involved a person is politically, the more likely her friends and acquaintances are to be politically active ás well. Social movements can build their own networks. And if you do come to a rally alone, it turns out you will soon find others to talk to, since people tend to welcome any participants. They are in a good mood.

On rare occasions entire networks can be recruited intact, in what is known as **bloc recruitment**: if a preacher joins the anti-abortion or civil rights movement, she can rent buses and bring many of her flock to a rally or to lobby legislators. The stronger the pre-existing networks, as with clans, castes, or peasant villages, the easier bloc recruitment is. Many Muslim demonstra-tions emerge naturally from Friday services in the local mosque. Religions spend generations building exactly the kind of positively charged networks that political activists dream of: why not try to energize them for your own cause?

Not everyone in a network rushes to join their friends at a dem-onstration, as some individuals are more **biographically available** than others. This means that they are free from other commit-ments that might hinder them: jobs with demanding hours, young children at home who have to be fed, physical weaknesses that might prevent them from marching or standing for long periods. Your position in a network is not everything. You may be willing but not able.

In fact your network position is only the start. Networks only matter because of the cultural work they do through the feelings that sustain them and the information that flows through them. David Snow, one of the scholars who showed the importance of network contacts for recruitment, was quick to demonstrate that information needs to be framed in the right way for it to have an impact (Snow et al. 1986). New recruits must see the relevance of an issue, understand its origins, and feel enough enthusiasm to do something about it. Snow and his collaborators developed the language of **frame alignment** to explain recruitment, as organizers and recruiters have to "align" their respective "frames" by linking new issues to social problems that people already care about. Networks transmit cultural meanings.

Nor is biographical availability a structural constraint, but an interpretation of the costs of participation. Having young kids impedes involvement only for those who let it; others bring their children along to protests. Not only are they teaching their chil-dren about protest and about issues, but for some, their children are at the heart of their cause. Anti-abortion activists bring their children to accent their family values, as do same-sex couples who desire for their children the same legal connections to *both* parents that other kids have, again demonstrating the importance of family. Organizers often establish childcare facilities so that parents can attend meetings.

Recruiting

A study of the anti-abortion movement shows how these network attachments work. Ziad Munson (2009), when he interviewed dozens of activists, was surprised to find that most of them did not have clear anti-abortion positions when they first joined; some were even mildly pro-choice. Their ideological positions developed over time, as they read the arguments, saw the films, and heard the speeches. Munson's explanation combines biographical availability (many had changed their lives in some way that freed up time, such as a move or a divorce) with network contacts (they went to a protest with a new acquaintance). Our attractions to other humans are a powerful guiding force in our actions.

This is an important general point: we do not walk around with elaborate ideologies to assess each political position that we encounter. But we do have subtle, often unconscious feelings about the world around us, especially the people around us. We trust some more than others, we admire some, love some (either platonically or lustfully). These affective orientations help us develop more elaborate views. We also have moral intuitions about right and wrong: we fear the massive radiation of nuclear power plants, able to reach inside us and generate cancer without our ever seeing it, but we need an occasion to nurture these feelings into an ideology of democracy against technocracy. It takes time to "learn" an issue.

Stories, which are often used in recruitment, also show the importance of our emotional orientations. Recruiters tell their own stories, but also encourage potential recruits to tell their stories, in the process hopefully seeing that their own experiences are not unusual but part of a broader pattern they share with others. (This was how feminist consciousness-raising groups worked.) A story engages us when we like the storyteller, when we trust her or at least sympathize with her. Part of that sympathy comes from the story itself, but it can also be there from the start, if we know the person already, or if she seems like someone we would trust if we did know her. Her reputation or charismatic presence may give her an initial dose of authority before she even mounts the podium, an act that yields even more authority.

Networks aid mobilization in other ways, giving members access to positions and resources that they can bring to the movement. Knowing wealthy people may help you raise funds, just as holding official positions brings the authority to dispense resources or make decisions. Many members of the lesbian and gay communities work in the media and cultural industries, such as theater and television, Hollywood and the visual arts, so when the movement radicalized in the mid-1980s it was extremely creative in its use of visual images. In another arena, GLAAD (the Gay and Lesbian Alliance against Defamation) was very effective in changing American television images. The mid-1990s saw an explosion of prime-time gays and lesbians, from Rickie on *My So-Called Life* and *Ellen* in 1994 to *Will and Grace* in 1998. To some extent these characters built on the very caring images that had emerged several years earlier during the AIDS crisis. It still took hard work and pressure from within the industry to create complex, sympathetic characters like these, a kind of normalizing, de-demonizing character work that is almost the opposite of a moral shock: gay people are not so shocking. (It is an important civil right, I suppose, to be able to mock your own group in silly prime-time sitcoms.)

As we'll see in later chapters, networks are not used only for recruiting new members, but also for retaining old ones, spreading information, and organizing events. This is no surprise, since all human life takes place through social networks.

Moral shocks

Not everyone is recruited to a movement through existing networks. A person may experience something that so upsets them – a **moral shock** – that they deeply want to get involved. They may go online to find help, seek out organizations in their community, or in extreme cases even start their own group. Mothers against Drunk Driving (MADD) chapters are created by women who have been struck by unbelievable tragedy, notably losing a child, and they somehow turn their grief into a determination to fix a

Rickie was not the central character in *My So-Called Life*, but he was a complex and sympathetic friend. Credit: Disney © Mark Selinger/American Broadcasting Companies, Inc.

problem. Sometimes political action is the most healing response to this mood of desperation. Doing something, almost anything, feels better than doing nothing.

An emotional state of shock gets people's attention. It can paralyze them, or it can develop into anger and indignation and propel them to action. A number of scholars have shown that moral shocks help recruit new people to movements, giving them a sense of urgency (Warren 2010). Activists try to generate moral transformations through their own propaganda, offering alarming images of suffering or stories of cruelty and oppression. But on occasion the vicissitudes of life itself push people into outraged action without much activist intervention. The unnecessary death of a loved one, whether from AIDS or drunk driving, is an especially strong prod to action.

The extension dilemma

Lest we get carried away with the recruitment power of networks, and assume that it is always better to recruit more and more members, the extension dilemma suggests that there are advantages to small, well-focused movements or groups as well. The larger a group or movement grows, the more likely there are to be disagreements over goals and tactics, for factions to form over these cleavages. The larger the movement, the harder it is to coordinate its actions and statements. A giant movement impresses, it gets attention, it compiles resources. But it is hard for it to maneuver. Strategic choices about *who* you will be as a movement entail choices about *what* you will do. Sometimes a small group or individual is more effective. You don't need a broad movement to hack corporate computers or sue discriminating employers.

I originally developed the term moral shock to get at the vertiginous, jittery feeling that results when something happens that shows you the world is not what you had thought, that someone is nastier, that a problem is more severe than you had ever imagined (Jasper 1997). Moral shocks rupture your sense of reality and normality, and sometimes lead to a thoroughgoing evaluation of your life and values. They are effective when they surprise us, when they offer us a sympathetic connection to other humans, and possibly when they allow us to express an emotion that we were not aware of beforehand. They usually help us understand our own feelings and moral intuitions; they do not impose new ones on us. As we probe our moral sensibilities, they may have implications we would hardly have expected.

There are milder versions of the same process, when we grow anxious about an issue and start paying closer attention to it. Political scientists, who have examined the emotions that help voters make their selections, argue that we are pushed out of our routines and into a **surveillance system** that scans the environment for novelty and threats, disrupting other activities until we evaluate the potential threat (Marcus 2002). We seek new information when we feel threatened, and we may change our habitual routines. We are prepared for action.

Although some shocks arise in personal life, others involve large numbers of people at the same time and are key **mobilizing moments** for activists. The most effective moral shocks probably come from dramatic public actions, when the police arrest, beat, and kill peaceful protestors, or when there is an oil spill or nuclear accident. In these cases, the public is already paying attention, and militants need only nudge them toward the right interpretation of the event (elites also try to shape our interpretations). When activists try to create their own moral shocks, they face a problem: what makes some audiences indignant and sympathetic may simply annoy the broader majority. Here we again see the innovation dilemma: go too fast in changing people's feelings, and you lose your audience; too slowly, and you don't get the changes you want.

Moral shocks are not only useful for understanding how someone is initially recruited to a movement; they also happen to seasoned activists in a way that revives or radicalizes their commitment. The *Hardwick* case helped lesbian and gay activists acknowledge their anger, and to realize that their quiet efforts to prove their own respectability had failed. They changed their approach to the naughty or nice dilemma. They had tried the nice route with little to show for it, and they had nothing left to lose from the naughty option. "*Hardwick*," concludes Gould (2009: 36), "by providing an unambiguous look at state homophobia, encouraged lesbians and gay men to channel blame and shame about AIDS away from themselves and toward the homophobic state and other institutions of society." The shock, indignation, and redirection of blame were powerful enough to push lesbians and gays into coalition with each other, after years of mostly separate social movements.

The naughty or nice dilemma

Protestors must often choose between tactics that are accepted or admired by authorities and the public, and tactics that are feared, despised, or at least disapproved of. Nice tactics bolster your reputation as morally upright, naughty tactics make you appear stronger and more threatening. Most social movements today take the moral high road, so it is easy to forget that naughty tactics can work in some circumstances. They heighten the risks: they may frighten or intimidate authorities and opponents into concessions, but they may also inspire repression, even lead to the end of the movement. Naughty tactics are most effective when there are important and relatively irreversible gains to be had, such as the right to vote, affirmative action programs, or union recognition. Some authors insist that the truly oppressed never make gains unless they intimidate and disrupt the status quo. Here's an example of naughty or nice from Occupy Oakland: anarchists had smashed the window of a coffee shop during a nocturnal clash with police. Another Occupier had attached a note: "We're sorry, this does not represent us." Beneath it, someone else had scrawled, "Speak for yourself."

Blame

Many of the cultural carriers we've seen – jokes, graffiti, characters, frames, stories, and more – are intended to find someone to blame for a problem. This is especially the rhetorical purpose of (blameworthy) villains and the (innocent) victims they harm. Mothers against Drunk Driving managed to capture both characters in their inspiring name: "mothers" implies the children who are killed, while "drunk drivers" are villains no one dares to defend.

Blame requires a social explanation of a problem as opposed to a natural one. We do not blame nature. If we frame a forest fire as the natural result of lightning, we are not likely to form a protest group. If we understand it as caused by arson, then we have a villain, although a criminal rather than a trigger for a social movement. But if we blame the fires on government policies of not clearing underbrush or of letting natural fires burn, then we have the cognitive and emotional components for protest blame. We have not only indignation (we can have that against the arsonist and other criminals), but a sense that governments should be held accountable.

Anita Bryant's campaign against gay rights, remarkably successful in the late 1970s, had to remake gay men into threatening villains: no easy feat. Her organization's name said it all: Save our Children. Her theme was that gays and lesbians were infiltrating the schools in order to prey on students and to turn them gay – homosexuality being an unnatural inclination that could only come from the outside, not from within people. She was reacting to a handful of gay rights ordinances that several cities had recently passed to prohibit discrimination, and her success at mobilizing the Christian Right made gay rights a national political issue around which the right mobilized quite successfully. The strategic dance between right and left continued, with each side's victories leading to countermobilization on the other side.

As different sides try to allocate blame, political struggles often address this boundary between what is natural and what is not. Many outcomes that we once accepted as natural catastrophes we now hope to be protected from. In the early 1980s, AIDS triggered a battle over blame. Christian fundamentalists were quick to condemn gay sex as "unnatural," insisting that these men were perpetrators, sinful villains instead of innocent victims. ACT UP emerged to fight this **blame structure:** instead, "people with AIDS" were victims of a virulent disease who deserved compassion, not the rightful recipients of God's wrath. The US government did not cause AIDS (although there were theories about this too), but it could be blamed for not funding enough research to fight the disease. The emaciated images of those dying victims aroused shock and pity, and the efforts of those caring for them were indeed heroic. ACT UP eventually won the character war, a crucial advance for gay rights.

Twenty years later, the issue of same-sex marriage proved surprisingly successful because it did not have to transform society's blame structures. There were no victims of same-sex marriage, even if a handful of hetero couples insisted that it might undermine the sanctity of their status. In story after news story, same-sex couples who had lived together for decades were overjoyed to be able to have a full marriage ceremony, often attended by their proud children. What could be more normal, even admirable? These cases contrasted with the negative examples, similar couples who were still not allowed to visit each other in the hospital or have any say at these important life events. The positive effects of same-sex marriage and the negative impact of its absence combined to form a powerful moral battery. Villains in this case were underplayed in favor of sympathetic victims, with archaic biblical prejudices as the source of injustice.

There is some tension between the demonization of particular people as the perpetrators of social problems and more abstract ideologies that trace problems to impersonal systems such as capitalism. Yet the best rhetoric combines the two. Ideologies are dry without personal examples, and individual villains are inexplicable without a theory of why they do bad things. The human mind grasps at vivid examples, and individuals and groups are the best kind, partly for the emotions we can feel about them. We needed the breathtaking criminal Bernie Madoff to epitomize the downfall of the financial system in 2008, destroyed by greedy, arrogant individuals at the top. Here was someone to despise. Only then, once we have these passionate symbols, do we add nuances such as global markets, regulatory (or in this case "deregulatory") regimes, and derivative financial instruments.

I said earlier that an irony of democracy is that our expectations for justice are higher, so that we have more occasions to protest. Our governments can be blamed for almost any calamity, not necessarily because they caused it but because they failed to anticipate it, warn or protect us, or fix the problem. State policies reach into almost all areas of our lives, from health epidemics to hazardous facilities to economic inequality, with many implied promises that government will take care of us. A central claim of the Occupy movement was that governments should intervene more to fix market outcomes; instead most governments have reduced – under the banner of austerity – even the mild redistribution they once accomplished through taxing and spending. The Occupiers tried to counter extensive corporate propaganda about markets being natural systems with their own laws, so that nobody can be blamed for their outcomes. Occupiers insisted that the 1 percent are to blame for restricting government as well as for bleeding the economy.

Threat

Villains grab our attention because negative emotions grab our attention, more immediately and urgently than positive emotions do. Most of the time, we live our lives through comfortable routines that require little attention, and it is mostly when dramatic or frightening events disrupt these routines that we pay attention to politics. Potential threats must be dealt with, which is why they startle us and give us a boost of adrenaline and cortisol. I call this **the power of negative thinking,** although it primarily involves the feelings that guide our attention and action. The demonization of villains, allocation of blame, indignation over victims: all these heighten our sense of threat and urgency.

But threat can also convey a sense of danger that prevents us from joining a protest movement. Governments usually dislike protestors, and if they can get away with it they usually send the police or the army to threaten or beat them. In repressive regimes, risks of bodily harm are the biggest deterrent to recruitment. If those risks are sufficient, all the social networks and character work in the world will not usually get people into the streets. Armies and police are better armed than protestors, even in the rare cases when those militants begin to form a revolutionary army. If the armed forces are willing to use those arms (a big if), they can keep killing protestors until none is left. The heroism of those willing to die for their ideals is extraordinary, something we should admire, but for that same reason we need to recognize that it is rare. We will look at repression more in chapter 7, especially to observe the emotional dynamics where, in some cases, repression leads to even greater mobilization rather than less. The pursuit of our indignant moral visions sometimes outweighs threats to our bodies.

Like fear more generally, a sense of threat can either paralyze us or propel us into action, what used to be known as fight-or-flight. In the face of repression, we often know that our own action is going to trigger even more repression, even worse situations. But sometimes we feel that our mobilization will work, and we may be talked out of our initial paralysis. This is what organizers try to do, to make the active option more appealing, less devastating. In moral shocks we are first stunned into inaction, and we often stay that way, but in some cases we see a path out through action. We often feel a great deal of tension when we are threatened but remain inert, and only vigorous action relieves that tension. Even if the action is dangerous, it is better than waiting for something to happen *to* us. It feels better to be active than passive.

Threats come in many forms, capable of inspiring protest: proposals for group homes for stigmatized groups like the homeless, people with AIDS, or foster children; techno-environmental risks like hazardous waste dumps, nuclear power plants, or incinerators; economic impacts such as unemployment, unsafe or unpleasant work conditions, or lack of respect by employers; diseases and medical procedures, such as AIDS, abortions, or low-grade silicone in breast implants; political infringements on our rights to assemble or to vote.

Protest movements have taught us to be suspicious of experts and government spokespersons who try to reassure us without providing all the facts. They often lie in order to prevent protests ("panic" as they erroneously call it, drawing on obsolete crowd theory), but their deception is what leads to even greater protest. In cases like these, people are going about their normal lives until a corporation or government decides on a threatening course of action.

Recruiting

Although some threats are to our physical well-being, such as a disease or a wage cut, most are attacks on our dignity. Even movements that appear to be about material conditions, such as the labor movement, are also about dignity, so that union recognition or reasonable work conditions are actually about respect. Economic protests like bread riots find human decisions to blame; they are not direct reactions to the price of bread. Brazilian protests in 2013 were partly in reaction to fare hikes in urban bus systems – a price that the government controls and could be held accountable for. Modern bread riots are also reactions to government decisions to increase or decontrol prices. Bus and bread prices may hurt, but not as much as the feeling of betrayal by our own government.

We see moral batteries here. We are fearful and angry about the negative situations or events which threaten us, and we admire and hope for the positive solutions that can save us. Like literal batteries, this combination separates the positive and the negative charges, giving us a direction in which to move. We are pulled toward the positive images and feelings. Moral batteries and moral shocks open people to their initial recruitment into a social movement.

* * *

We have looked at a number of mechanisms that get people involved in social movements. New ideas and causes get articulated in small groups, sometimes leading to recruitment efforts. These efforts turn first to existing social networks, but also try to build new ones. These networks are useful because they carry cultural meanings: moral shocks, moral batteries, blame structures, and a sense of threat and urgency. People must recognize a social problem, have faith that it can be fixed, and feel sufficient indignation to get involved. They must also trust the organizers who offer them a solution.

As we will see in the next chapter, the same kinds of mechanisms provide a constant source of motivation inside the movement, to keep people coming back, sometimes for life. Even those who have been recruited must have their commitment reinforced regularly, since there are always competing demands on their time and money. The same emotional processes that got them involved initially may keep them coming back, but additional factors also kick in. It is exciting to attend your first rally, but why do people come to their hundredth?

5

Sustaining

Not quite human: Dalit rights

"Untouchability" is based on disgust: another person's body is so dirty that it would harm you to touch it, to use the same sheets or dishes, to drink water from the same well, to breathe the same air. Even the untouchable's shadow might threaten your purity. This is a terrible form of oppression, especially since it is often linked to another form, slavery. Untouchable castes in India and neighboring nations have traditionally been restricted to occupations that their "superiors" could not perform without a sense of pollution: tanning hides, slaughtering animals, cleaning outhouses, and such. India sees thousands of attacks against Dalits (untouchables) every year, some of them fatal. Only in the last 100 years have India's Dalits dared to promote their rights against the dominant Brahmin Hinduism that places them in such a horrid status.

The 170 million Dalits in India and its neighboring countries face an extreme version of the **stigmatized-identity dilemma**: you are organizing to abolish negative stereotypes and identities, but you are mobilizing a movement based on those same tarnished identities. These are typically a source of shame, which you need to transform into pride, a sense of human dignity. African Americans, LGBTQ communities, the mentally ill, and many other groups have faced the same challenge. The first step is to adopt new, less offensive names. Just as "colored" Americans became negroes, Afro-Americans, blacks, and African Americans, so India's untouchables became Panchamas, scheduled castes, Harijan, and Dalits. The Dalit Panthers were formed in 1972 in recognition that the Black Panthers in the US had fostered enormous pride in being black, partly through shows of strength like carrying weapons. (This move from nice to naughty tactics generates pride at some cost, namely attacks by others: Dalits and Black Panthers are and were much more likely to be attacked than to attack anyone. But suffering from violence is more tolerable when accompanied by group pride.)

Affirmative action programs demonstrate the stigmatized-identity dilemma: these programs confer real benefits, especially university educations or jobs, but they highlight and make permanent the objectionable categories. Many castes debated whether to be included in India's affirmative-action schedule in the 1930s, which listed the castes to benefit, hence the "scheduled castes." These programs also arouse a backlash by those who feel they are losing advantages. In 1990, 200 Indian students set themselves on fire to protest new national quotas setting aside a certain number of university places for Dalits. Other upper-caste protestors set cars on fire, stopped trains, and boycotted classes. Self-assertion of a long-oppressed group infuriates those who have taken their own superiority for granted; it feels like an attack on their own pride and honor. Many Dalits, faced with the stigmatized-identity dilemma, move to cities, change their last names (which are typically caste-related), and seek individual advancement, avoiding any collective or individual efforts based on Dalit identity.

For those who choose a collective path, the challenge is to rework the shared identity in ways that encourage political participation. Sometimes this involves finding new audiences, who are unaware of or unmoved by the stigma, or perhaps are even sympathetic, such as international human rights groups that can intervene. Even more important is to alter the content of the identity. Groups that are seen as weak find symbols of strength; groups castigated as immoral seek ways to claim dignity and honor. Thus the leader of the Dalits in the early twentieth century was always called *Doctor* Ambedkar, much like *Doctor* Martin Luther King Jr. Because group identity is often based on a shared history, many

Dalit castes have embraced mythic figures as the founders of their caste, in the process repositioning themselves higher in the caste hierarchy by virtue of the founder's alleged occupation or lineage.

It is not easy being a Dalit, and it is not easy protesting as a Dalit. Organizers for Dalit rights have to offer reasons for people to continue in their movements once they have been recruited. There must be satisfactions along the way, as well as an awareness of the ultimate prize at the end. These gratifications include pride in a new positive identity and the immediate enjoyments of protesting in large groups. Organizations and their leaders have to keep such incentives in mind if they are to accomplish anything.

The pleasures of protest

People return to protest events again and again mostly because they enjoy them. They may relish the incomparable satisfaction of being a good person, of doing the right thing, for a cause they believe in completely. They also look forward to seeing old acquaintances, now comrades. Politics is a part of their lives, a habit they hardly need to think about.

But protests can also just be fun. Collective marching, singing, and shouting can be exhilarating, even when they entail some risk or fear. Large gatherings help relieve the tedium of routine activities such as writing letters, licking stamps, and making phone calls – although this too can be fun depending on who you're doing it with.

Meetings and rallies, any place where people come together, generate emotions (Collins 2001, 2004). Our bodies fall into rhythm with each other, and in addition to our awareness of each other we jointly focus our attention on the center of the gathering – the person speaking, the music, the physical symbols – and we feel excited. Just the close presence of others triggers many feeling-thinking processes. The result is a high of emotional energy that we associate with the gathering, the group that organized it, and the cause for which we are fighting. We are in a good mood, which persists for days or weeks after the event ends. When events go well, generating this energy, participants come to crave it. They will return.

People keep the good mood going a little longer by taking souvenirs with them, objects they can show to others that remind them of a special event. Videos are commonplace today, just as photos were a generation ago. T-shirts are pervasive: they are not only a souvenir, but an advertisement to others, and a way to increase the look and feel of solidarity among a crowd at the event itself. A sea of yellow or red proves the solidarity of a group.

Festivals, when crowds gather outside the usual routines of daily life, naturally put people in festive moods. The world is on holiday, a joyous bivouac. India is known for its frequent festivals, or melas, and so Dalit pride leaders have created their own melas or taken over existing ones. The oldest of the new melas is Ambedkar Jayanti in Agra, which began in 1957, the year after Ambedkar's death, as a commemoration including feasts, games, and speeches, and culminating in a seven-hour parade. Participants buy new clothes, prepare special meals, and invite relatives to visit. Drama and painting, debate and essay writing contests, fireworks and firecrackers, and free medical clinics all enhance the festivals. Celebrations like these are not explicitly political, or not always, but they reinforce fond feelings of Dalit identity.

Gatherings like these put people in good moods, energize them, and connect them with each other, a process that inspired crowd theory. Driven by their fears of working-class crowds, elite intellectuals saw the effects of crowds as inevitably bad: anger, fear, then violence. They largely ignored the enthusiasm, solidarity, and calm concentration of which crowds are also capable. Participants come to share the same emotions because emotions are contagious: when we see someone smile, we usually smile too, and we begin to feel happy as a result. We can become angry through the same kind of **emotional contagion.** Crowds often share reflex emotions because the police make arrests, beat several people, or act in some other way that sparks anger. In other words, members of a crowd interact with each other but also with outsiders.

Nothing generates a good mood like a sense of momentum, the feeling that we can't lose, that everything is going our way.

Victories provide this confidence, especially victories that follow a loss or two. Even a series of larger and larger marches or rallies can suggest momentum, a kind of internal victory of recruitment that surely will lead to external victories against opponents or the government. The grandest sense of momentum comes from a historical narrative that has a special place for your movement as the harbinger of social change and justice to come. The Christian Right, for instance, was sustained by the certainty that God's eternal justice would eventually triumph. A narrative like this can sometimes even be a salve for current setbacks, ridicule, or lack of interest: these will ultimately be reversed. A sense of **making history** is about as satisfying as life gets. (Grand historical narratives may not work as theoretical explanations, but they work well as political rhetoric.)

Events can go badly, too. They are broken up by the police, sometimes violently. Or, perhaps worse, they feel routine and dull. If they fail to hold our attention, small groups start talking to each other instead of listening to the speakers. People drift away, draining the energy of those who remain. Or perhaps no outsiders pay attention, there is no media coverage, no one else thinks what we are doing is important. We begin to worry about that ourselves. If attendance is lower than we expected, we worry that the movement has lost momentum and is going into decline.

There are other kinds of meetings, with different emotional effects. A small weekly or monthly meeting of familiar faces, in a kitchen or living room, has the warm feel of family, so different from big media events, which are harder to plan and pull off and so are less frequent, but have the potential excitement of influencing the world. Movements tend to offer both kinds of moments. If there were only small meetings, it might feel as if the group were too tiny or inward-looking. If there were only large events, aimed outward, there might not be enough internal solidarity to keep people returning. Movements have learned something from successful religions, most of which have daily or weekly services for the community as well as thrilling annual festivals or once-in-a-lifetime pilgrimages. Today's most successful Dalit politician, Mayawati, who ran the Indian state of Uttar Pradesh off and on for nearly 20 years, built hundreds of towering statues of Dalit ancestors and leaders, including many of herself, throughout Uttar Pradesh, in the hopes that they would become pilgrimage sites.

As we saw in chapter 2, moving together by dancing or marching is an extreme form of the mutual entrainment of face-to-face gatherings, and the resulting mood can reach ecstatic joy, the feeling that you are a small part of a vast whole. Music and chants complete this sense of total envelopment. Participants can be charged up to sacrifice themselves, or they may simply feel awe and love for the group. Fatigue, thirst, and hunger fade in importance, in much the same processes that religions use to create altered states of consciousness.

Most protest is not this exciting, however, and requires other incentives. Foremost is a sense of belonging and obligation to one's group.

Collective identity

A central motive for participating in a movement is a feeling of identification with the group it claims to represent, or with the movement itself. Some movements emerge from a pre-existing **collective identity**, much as the US civil rights movement grew naturally out of the African American population, or the gay and lesbian rights movement aims to represent its community. Movement leaders, in these cases, do not need to create new identities, they need to reinterpret existing ones. To be a full member of the LGBTQ community meant marching in the streets against AIDS policies; it meant going to ACT UP meetings. A successful group manages to associate itself with the collective identity closely enough to attract many members of the group.

Not all collective identities are based on pre-existing traits like race-ethnicity or gender. Movements form their own identities as well. These **movement identities** can be based on organizational membership or adherence to tactics, or they can draw on the solidarity that arises out of an inspiring sense of a national or international effort. When an individual identifies with a group, her loyalty helps to keep her involved. As the innovation dilemma suggests, it is usually harder to create a new collective identity than to hijack an existing one, but it is not impossible. Dalit leaders are trying to do just this: to overcome individual caste identities in favor of a broader Dalit label, which in the past had been imposed by outsiders (by Brahmins originally and by government programs more recently).

No group ever attains complete homogeneity, and subgroups often complain that their visions and interests are being ignored. No sooner had the women's movement emerged in the US in the late 1960s than black and Latino women complained that it did not speak for them; lesbians also felt excluded (no wonder: Friedan called them "the lavender menace" that would discredit the women's movement). More specific identities, such as black working-class lesbians, also feel better to some members of that category than to others. Every collective identity is a *necessary fiction*: it is necessary for recruitment in most cases, and for making demands on authorities in many, but it is always a fiction in that it papers over so many differences between individuals (Gamson 1995). For that reason a lot of recent groups have studiously avoided all identity claims, swinging to the opposite end of the tradeoff.

Stigmatized identities, we saw, pose a variation of the identity dilemma. The same group stereotypes that you are trying to combat also help form the identity you are using to recruit. You might wish to live in a world where no one much cares about anyone's caste background, but you would have a hard time building a movement in that world. In this world, however, you can recruit those who have been taunted with nasty names, violently attacked, spurned by their neighbors, and given a cold shoulder by coworkers, in other words those with anger and indignation.

The two great collective identities of the last 200 years, nation and class, were initially promoted by social movements. *Nations* are one of the most successful collective identities of all time, and all the cultural tools we have seen were used to create them: long historical narratives, shared printed languages, markets for disseminating newspapers and novels, sentimental paintings of

The identity dilemma

The promotion of a collective identity poses risks as well as benefits for a social movement (McGarry and Jasper 2015). It energizes those who feel enthusiastic about the identity: those who wear it well. But it turns off others who are uncomfortable with it. (They may still participate, even if they feel indifferent or cynical about the identity, if they think that it may be useful strategically.) In movements based on strong collective identities, we often see a continual splitting as one subgroup after another decides to march under its own banner. The women's movement fragmented by race-ethnicity and sexual orientation; the lesbian liberation movement then split into the LGBT movements; "queer" movements emerged in the 1990s to challenge *all* collective identities on the grounds that they distort people's sense of self by imposing an "essence" on them. In response, many transsexuals insist that they *do* have an essential inner self that is distorted by society's prejudices. The dilemma continues. The challenge is to find the symbols and formulations that attract whom you want (this is not necessarily the largest number, as the extension dilemma tells us). When an identity is stigmatized, an individual may feel that she can live a better life by distancing herself from her identity – through assimilation or passing – instead of embracing it through political action.

landscapes and peasants, adapted folksongs – and of course artistic, political, and military movements that fought to make "the people" and their government line up. Nationalism has been a favorite vision of people who lack proper nations, such as today's Palestinians, but it has also sent millions of young people off to war to defend their nation's honor. And like every collective identity, it disqualified many alternative identities: women were usually excluded from militaristic versions, racial-ethnic minorities from biologically based stories, immigrants from historical narratives. As the identity dilemma suggests, every inclusion is also an exclusion.

The band of brothers dilemma

For a group or movement to last, its members need to feel some emotions of solidarity: pride, trust, love, excitement, respect, and more. So movements and organizations try to inspire these feelings through symbols and activities. But these affective loyalties do not always attach themselves to the *right* group. Instead of identifying with the whole movement, individuals may instead come to love the members of their immediate affinity group or small organization. Face-to-face bonds can crowd out the larger group, and if there is conflict between the broader identity and the narrower one, the latter usually wins. Organizations pull out of coalitions; affinity groups move intact to new movements. The Dalit movement has tried hard to build solidarity across the lower castes, but often it has instead bolstered the pride of particular castes, who have used it to climb the caste ladder at the expense of fellow Dalit castes.

Class was the other great identity of the last 200 years, and the working class in particular was a necessary fiction that created socialist and labor parties with an enormous impact on policies in many countries. Like nationalism, its great competitor, socialism spawned an elaborate ideology and rich cultural traditions. Innumerable movements have claimed to represent the working class, just as nationalists claimed to represent "the people." (*Populism* combines elements of both, claiming to speak for the people in contrast to rich, corrupt, parasitic, alien elites.) When the Great War began in Europe in 1914, national identities generally proved more appealing than class identities, and socialist leaders were appalled to see so many of their members enlist enthusiastically in capitalist, imperialist warfare.

Activist tourism, an old practice that has recently been given this new name, depends on a sense of comradeship with an imagined community of fellow activists, so that people travel to see what others are up to. A generation ago an occasional German tourist-activist would show up at the office of the antinuclear

Abalone Alliance in San Francisco; in recent years the majority of cyclists at New York's Critical Mass gatherings have been out-of-towners hoping to experience the thrill of this famous monthly bicycle ride/protest. Each visit depends on an imagined movement, against nuclear energy or automobiles, for example, with sufficient shared values that would make a visitor feel welcome. And she usually is welcome. As inevitably happens with successful ideas, corporations adapted it, so that you can go on "activist tours" of the rainforest or impoverished countries, doing a little ecological research and talking to locals. Governments too got into the act, with the Israeli government in particular funding "homeland" or "birthright" pilgrimages by 10–20,000 young diaspora Jews each year, the last remnant of nineteenth-century-style national identity construction (Kelner 2010).

Groups and organizations

Groups and organizations actively create and manage most of the techniques we have seen for imparting loyalty and enthusiasm, such as networks, identities, and the pleasures of protest. Leaders know that their groups would not be able to function without this apparatus, and, as we saw in chapter 3, organizations are the primary backbone of most protest movements. They keep them going.

Organizations help us think as well as telling us what to do. They allow decision-making in some areas but discourage it in others, leaving many possible strategic choices out of bounds. This is useful, in fact unavoidable, since not everything can be put on the table at all times without leading to full-time discussion, as was almost reached in Occupy's unwieldy General Assemblies. We tend to accept as common sense those decisions or practices that are not open for debate: they are just the way things are. In their first few months of existence, protest groups create a number of rules that can then be taken for granted and not revisited in future meetings (Blee 2012). Organizations produce explicit mission statements and arguments, but they also send messages through their structures. A participatory structure suggests that democracy is both an important goal and also, even if cumbersome at times, ultimately effective.

Many scholars talk about **organizational cultures**, suggesting particular ways of thinking and feeling that all or most members share. Since organizations can also turn into contentious arenas very easily, I am not so sure we should emphasize what they share. Any gathering of individuals, no matter how much enthusiasm they feel for the group, is going to share many beliefs and feelings but disagree over others. The balance between agreement and disagreement shifts constantly and unexpectedly.

This does not stop organizational leaders from *trying* to create homogeneity in their groups. Those who disagree vociferously (especially when they disagree with the leaders) or who otherwise cause trouble can be purged, an expulsion that can be accomplished nicely or not so nicely. There are also subtle pressures for group conformity; it never feels good to be the only dissenting voice in a group for which you have positive feelings. The band of brothers tradeoff appears here: it is easier to question the official line if you are part of a small dissenting group, and much harder if you are totally alone in your disagreement. Groups and organizations that endure usually manage to build up a shared vision to some degree, else they would not survive. Like collective identities, this agreement is a necessary fiction.

Two kinds of feelings contribute to group solidarity. The obvious one consists of the **reciprocal emotions** that group members feel for each other: respect, love, admiration, trust, and more – along with some fractious feelings like jealousy or betrayal. But solidarity is also affected by the **shared emotions** that group members feel toward outsiders, events, and so on. Sharing a feeling – everyone in the group hates nuclear energy or caste hierarchy – also makes them feel better about each other: these people also hate castes, so they must be kindhearted, sensible, admirable. Shared emotions usually arise from shared experiences, as when an affinity group is pepper-sprayed, arrested, and spends time in jail together. Even unpleasant experiences can build solidarity. Dalits, LGBTs, or racial-ethnic groups derive solidarity, alas, from being treated in nasty ways. We saw the same two sources of feelings with crowds, in which members interact with each other (forming reciprocal emotions), as with outside players such as the police (forming shared emotions).

Groups try hard to arouse loyalties in members, so that they enjoy being with the group, so that membership is part of their identity, so that they like or love other members, are proud of what the group does, trust it to make the right decisions, and adopt the right tactics. In a word, they have an organizational collective identity. There can always be too much of a good thing, of course, and groups can become sects, sealed off from the world, if this solidarity overwhelms other goals. They can run afoul of the Janus dilemma. But strong group solidarity need not turn inward; it can also encourage heroic efforts in fighting external battles against the group's foes.

Groups, or more specifically their leaders, have a number of techniques for creating this kind of loyalty (Lalich 2004). Belief systems instill a sense of higher purpose and meaning, a feeling of collective efficacy, and hope for the future. Groups offer something to do, organizing members' lives, providing a feeling of security in the group, giving them a sense of accomplishment, and also – when the groups are all-encompassing – meeting daily personal needs and offering a sense of justice within the group. A strong group gives a sense of belonging and comradeship, members are moral role models for each other, and they develop a sense of being part of something greater. Members feel renewed, born again. As always, these benefits can reach toxic extremes of self-righteous dogmatism, totalizing worldviews closed to new evidence, imbalanced lives, anxiety and guilt over not doing enough, and – ultimately – burnout.

Another risk of strong group loyalty is that members' goals and leaders' goals begin to diverge, so that leaders try to use members' commitment to get them to do things they never intended or wanted.

Leaders

Leaders emerge in almost any social setting, whether or not an organization is structured to give them official positions. It's not necessarily that they talk more, but people respect what they say. They come up with good ideas, and make them work. Leaders even appear in groups that rotate positions, give everyone an equal voice, and undertake other measures designed to prevent the emergence of leaders. Yet they do emerge. The word "leadership" has a kind of aura in some societies, especially the United States, thanks to military and business literatures that suggest we should idolize and obey the charismatic few who can "get things done." We don't need to go to that mystical extreme to acknowledge that certain people take charge (they may not always be the ones we expect).

Let's call these people **decisive leaders**, who have either official positions or informal respect that allows them to mobilize resources, demand others' attention, and speak for an organization. Their choices and arguments tend to have more influence than other people's. To understand how a specific protest unfolds, we would like to know something about decisive leaders' goals, their knowledge and experience, their interpretation of the world generally and of the immediate situation particularly, their feelings about different tactical options, their patterns of trust and mistrust for other players, and dozens of more subtle factors that go into their decisions. So subtle that the decisive leaders themselves can never articulate all their reasons, for their experience has given them an intuitive sense of what will work at any given moment, of how to balance long- and short-run objectives, of how to deal with dozens of strategic dilemmas, often several intertwined dilemmas at the same time. An effective leader feels her way through many decisions, even though she takes in information from others, gives her best reasons, and defends her actions afterward.

Leaders play a second role, as symbols of a group, movement, or moral vision. With these **symbolic leaders** their own decisions may not matter. They can remain or become symbolic leaders even after they are dead and incapable of making earthly choices, because it is really other people who do most of the work in crafting their reputations, interpreting their actions and intentions, and generally using an individual in the same way they would any other symbol or image (Fine 2001). It is often the news media that create symbolic leaders, making them familiar to new audiences and interpreting (often misinterpreting, in the eyes of the movement) what they mean. They may be a symbol to members of the movement, to outside audiences, or to both. Symbolic leaders embody what a movement is fighting for, and how. Gandhi was a powerful symbol of nonviolent resistance to imperialism, embodying in his clothes, his posture, and his tiny size a fighter who was frail yet tough, an underdog who would endure. As the novelist John Dos Passos said of socialist leader Eugene Debs, he "made them want the world he wanted."

Not all human symbols epitomize a movement; some embody the social problem the movement is trying to fix. Victims of domestic abuse, for instance, can be resonant symbols who express urgency, but their victimhood prevents them from being symbolic leaders. There are cases in between these, too: Rosa Parks was a victim who helped inspire a movement by choosing to do something different one day. She symbolized resistance, without being represented as a decisive leader of the civil rights movement (although she was actually more involved in decision-making than the symbolic victim myth implies).

As the Rosa Parks case suggests, there are a number of tensions possible between the roles of decisive and of symbolic leaders. Most leaders are both, but their performances in the two roles can interfere, and few carry out each of them equally well. In some cases this reflects the Janus dilemma, as a leader can be a good internal manager but unappealing as the face of the movement to the outside world. In other cases, their very success as decision-makers makes them unsuitable symbols, for instance when they adopt unsavory means, perhaps violence, that are unpalatable to most other players and audiences. Some of the most successful leaders are famous for dying well: just at the moment when they cease being decisive leaders they do something that will make them better symbolic leaders. This is the symbolic power of martyrs, who die for the cause, although not all martyrs are decisive individuals before their deaths. Some become known symbolically only through their deaths.

Leaders can function as symbols long after they are dead.

Religious figures like Mohammed or Buddha are the obvious examples, but Macedonians are still proud of Alexander the Great, the Dutch of William the Silent. They are central to the founding myths of groups and nations. B. R. Ambedkar, known fondly as Babasaheb, led the movement for Dalit rights from the 1920s until his death in 1956. His central strategy was mass conversion to Buddhism, which does not recognize castes, but he succeeded with only a tiny proportion of Dalits. When politicians wish to appease or appeal to Dalit voters, they name a university or airport after Ambedkar, even posthumously awarding him a Bharat Ratna, India's highest civilian honor, in 1990. Stories about and memorials to him are central to programs to create Dalit pride. He has been deified.

Charisma is the term often used to capture the supposed mystery of leadership, and it refers to a special type of symbolic leader, who is a strong symbol to her own movement members. They trust her to make the right decisions, to have good intentions, to see things that others cannot. They will follow her into battle, figuratively if not literally, in the belief that she will protect them and lead them to victory through her special powers. Outsiders may not share this view of the charismatic leader, although internal and external reputations typically interact. They usually support one another, but not always. In character terms, insiders and outsiders are more likely to agree on a leader's strength or weakness than on whether she is good or bad. Charisma is often said to result from an interaction between an individual and the situation that thrusts her into prominence, sometimes despite her initial reluctance, but we should not forget that personal qualities continue to matter. Not every individual rises to the occasion.

During the group interactions that generate emotions, such as festivals, some people are at the center and some are on the periphery. Those at the center of the ceremony gain charisma because the members of the group associate them with the excitement and energy they feel. The charismatic leaders, buoyed by the attention, also experience those emotions more strongly, often feeling as if they have been possessed by a power greater than themselves.

Whether we call the process charisma or not, what happens

when a group's member comes to see its leader as embodying its highest moral vision and goals? The leader lends the member a sense of purpose, of belonging to a community, a feeling of security because the leader knows what she is doing. The member may simply be intrigued by the leader, who is a bit distant and mysterious, and the leader may make him feel special, among the chosen few. Feelings like these, unfortunately, give the leader great latitude to break the rules and indulge in autocratic whims. The leader, as the embodiment of the group, must be defended at all costs. How can you question a leader you expect to be perfect and special, innovative and unique?

One risk is that leaders substitute their own goals and interests for those of the group. The stronger the leaders – or their organizations – the more they develop their own goals, producing a cluster of strategic dilemmas. But blatant personal corruption does not always harm a leader's reputation with her followers. Mayawati, the charismatic teacher-turned-politician, was investigated frequently for corruption, based on the dramatic disparity between her known income and her accumulated wealth. Journalists and national politicians disliked her, but the corruption inquiries (which never resulted in formal charges) did not trouble her supporters. Undoubtedly, many Dalits were proud that one of their own was feeding at the trough at long last. Her lavish spending on statues of herself, presented to innumerable villages around Uttar Pradesh, had the same effect. She also shared the wealth, using the incentives available to an old-fashioned party machine: jobs, free bicycles, publicly financed houses, and cheap electricity, which arrived in many villages for the first time.

Movement decline

We have seen a lot of ways that movements recruit newcomers and retain oldsters, but there comes a time for every movement when none of that works any more. A movement may decline fast, in the face of repression or sometimes because it has won a great victory, or it may decline slowly, depressingly, with one person

A new hero is constructed: for Mayawati, helping herself and helping her people are the same thing. Credit: © AP Photo/Tsering Topgyal.

after another failing to show up to the next event. The pleasures of protest begin to feel shallow; collective identities fragment or lose their thrill; organizations ossify; leaders become autocrats or defect. All the mechanisms that sustain protest begin to reverse themselves.

Disagreements over strategic dilemmas begin to pile up, leaving bitter feelings between factions. Conversely, a sour mood of decline makes each strategic choice seem more important, worth fighting for, as if that choice might save the movement. The Amsterdam squatters' movement in its final stages was caught irreconcilably on the naughty or nice dilemma, pitting those who wished to confront the state with violence against those who saw this as a disastrous strategy (Owens 2009). A predictably gendered division arose, with men wanting to fight and women wanting to protect the homes they had built, and each side blamed the other for the setbacks. The naughty camp tried to address its fears through radical action; the nice camp fell back on the internal solidarities of the group and tried to withdraw from public confrontation.

Movements rarely disappear completely. Some leave behind interest groups that subsist on contributions from former enthusiasts. Others persist as a tiny sect. The National Women's Party endured for decades, between one wave of the women's movement and the next, by closing in on itself (Rupp and Taylor 1987). The handful of members were devoted to its charismatic leader, tied to each other through strong emotional, and in some cases romantic, bonds. The group was more cult than party, despite the name, and its exclusive, hierarchical structure actually helped it last, even though it did not help it recruit new members. It was forced to follow an extreme strategy in the face of the Janus dilemma, but this worked.

* * *

All sorts of motives keep a movement going: the thrill of coordinated crowds and festivals, the pride in belonging to a strong or good group, the pleasures of seeing old friends and making new ones. Groups and organizations set up the actions that help us feel these things, and sometimes they become a new source of collective pride. Leaders devote the most energy to these efforts, in part because they get the most out of them. As they get more powerful, they can help the group enormously – or help themselves instead. Yet all these solidarities and excitements can turn sour, and when they do the movement is in trouble.

Assembling and retaining a team is crucial to a group or movement, but the team must also decide what they are going to do. There are lots of different ways to make choices. And none of them guarantees that the decisions will always be good ones.

6

Deciding

Riots and forums: the global justice movement

Before Occupy there was the global justice movement, a network
of groups fighting US-style capitalism, also known as neoliberalism
for its enthusiasm for "free markets." With roots in debates over
the North American Free Trade Agreement (NAFTA) between
the US, Mexico, and Canada, and inspired by the Zapatistas in
Mexico who formed to oppose NAFTA on the first day of 1994,
the global justice movement crystalized in 1999, when large protests shut down the streets of Seattle and – as a result – the World
Trade Organization meeting. Media coverage was enormous,
partly because this happened in the US (there had been prior protests against neoliberal policies in Latin America and elsewhere),
and partly because some shop windows were smashed (in response
to police use of pepper spray, tear gas, and concussion bombs).
The Seattle police added to the attention by claiming, falsely,
that protestors had thrown Molotov cocktails at them. Naughty
tactics – whether blocked streets or broken windows – get noticed.

The global justice movement concentrated on two main tactics:
disrupting economic summit meetings like the one in Seattle, and
holding its own counterforums. Beginning with the first World
Social Forum in Porto Alegre, Brazil in 2001, there was a prolif-
eration of social forums at the levels of continents, nations, and
cities. Inspired partly by social theory about good, undistorted

communication, and in reaction to elite meetings of the World Economic Forum, the World Social Forums have brought together thousands of groups opposed to corporate capitalism and especially to efforts by the US government to impose it on other nations. They continue today.

After Seattle the anti-summit protestors fiercely debated the use of violent tactics such as battling the police and breaking windows. Since there was no way to restrain those who believed in property damage, organizing groups eventually agreed to allow room for different kinds of groups to use their own tactics, to elaborate on their own versions of opposition to rampant capitalism, and to coordinate their actions without needing to agree on principles (della Porta et al. 2006). In contrast, the forums were about communication, agreement, and decision-making. They turned out to be a laboratory for democratic innovation.

At the beginning, the forums declared that they would proceed by consensus, derived from nonviolence and the kind of participatory democracy that was supposed to prefigure the ideal future society. Disagreements quickly arose between Marxists, whose historical theory told them what the most effective decisions should involve (seizing the state, attacking economic power), and those who believed that the *process* of decision-making was most important, no matter what decisions followed from it. The latter group soon adopted the identity of "horizontalists," in order to criticize the "verticalists" from communist parties and trade unions. These "old left" groups were powerful allies for the movement, with the dilemma they pose. The verticalists pointed out that too much attention to internal process would leave less time for external engagements with the powerful. (We saw the same Janus dilemma with Occupy.)

Disagreements also emerged over the meaning of consensus (Maeckelbergh 2009). Many assumed that it meant that differences had to be reconciled in order to reach unanimous opinions and decisions. With enough time and goodwill, unanimity was possible; a new identity for the group would emerge from the process. Others pointed out that this level of agreement was simply not possible in diverse movements, and that claims to consensus would really just paper over fundamental disagreements.

The powerful allies dilemma

Strategic players often align with others who have resources, political connections, know-how, and access to audiences. Through these sources of power you can advance the interests of your movement. But of course these allies have their own goals as well, which never line up perfectly with your goals. They can use their power to twist your movement to suit their own needs just as easily as they can use their power on your behalf. A politician may take on your cause, for example, but in the process reinterpret it so that it seems to support her own favorite proposal. Established parties and politicians usually have a moderating effect on a movement's demands. Celebrities, unions, foundations, and the media are also potential allies who pose this dilemma. (The media dilemma is closely related.)

Individuals and even small groups would feel pressured to go along with the "consensus." This is the same issue we saw with collective identities: they are necessary fictions, and are never going to fit everyone perfectly well. In the new view, consensus meant cooperating despite difference, recognizing that social life will always contain conflict and difference. The only agreement among all participants was opposition to global capitalism, as reflected in the slogan, "one no, many yeses."

Thanks to the identity politics of the previous generation of activists, forum organizers were well aware that certain demographic groups – based on race-ethnicity, class, gender, and sexual orientation – might need special encouragement to participate. But having sufficient numbers from different groups was not enough; they needed the confidence and skills to contribute fully, such as a persuasive language for giving speeches to large audiences. In a similar experiment in democracy, translators occasionally intervened to insist that certain voices be more fully heard, bringing proceedings to a temporary halt in order to focus attention on this issue (Doerr 2012).

Protest groups have wonderfully diverse mechanisms for

deciding what to do, ranging from steep pyramids where a small circle of leaders make all the decisions, to ultra-participatory groups that welcome everyone to their assemblies – even strangers off the street in the case of Occupy Wall Street. From the outside, a protest group or organization may look like a unified player with a plan, a tactic, a program, but when we look inside it we always see that it is also an arena where there can be enormous conflict among the individuals and factions who make it up. All strategic players have this characteristic: they are arenas as well as players.

Routines and creativity

We saw that protestors typically rely on a small repertory of familiar tactics, doing the same things over and over, because their meanings are understood by participants and by external audiences. For Charles Tilly, who developed this idea, repertories were initially a structural concept, meant to show that protestors had to adapt to the political arenas available to them if they hoped to succeed. Over time he acknowledged more and more of the cultural determinants of repertories: protestors choose tactics that seem morally righteous to them; they rely on their own know-how, usually derived from individuals' experience in other movements. Protestors change their repertories through their interactions with other players, anticipating others' moves, trying to surprise others, and innovating when blocked (Krinsky and Barker 2009).

Innovation of any kind is hard to understand, but we certainly never get there from a structural orientation: structures have no reason to change, except for the occasional, unpredictable shock from the outside. Yet political arenas are changing constantly. To understand this we need to grasp people's own points of view, seeing what goals they have, so that we can see what they are willing to give up when things are not going well. Even when a group seems – to outside observers – to be failing, members may insist that success is just around the corner, even as its numbers shrink, the mood turns sour, and the rest of the world stops paying attention. There are no clear standards to judge how successful a group is, so it can believe it is having an impact even when there is not much objective evidence for it.

One reason groups stick with the same tactical choices is that our tactics are never a neutral question about what will work; all tactics have moral implications of some kind. Nonviolent groups would not embrace violence even if it guaranteed victory; working-class groups may feel more comfortable marching together on a picket line than lobbying their legislators one on one; a group of lawyers will concentrate on legal procedures and avoid breaking the law. Different people have different **tastes in tactics**, favoring some tactics over others in almost all circumstances. They may cling to their favored activities even when they are not working well. Tastes in tactics help explain why innovation is rare; they reinforce existing repertories.

Some innovation comes from new variations on existing tactics. Nonviolent theorist Gene Sharp (2012) has counted the tactics available to protestors, finding a couple hundred distinct actions and variations – and these are just the nonviolent tactics. For example, under psychological interventions (Sharp distinguishes interventions from non-cooperation), he mentions self-exposure to the elements, fasting, reverse trials (putting the powerful on mock trial), and nonviolent harassment; under physical interventions – forms of occupation – he lists sit-ins, stand-ins, ride-ins, wade-ins, mill-ins, and pray-ins. Some of these tactics are rarely used due to current tastes in tactics or their lack of impact, but others have simply been forgotten. Creative groups can revive them, catching their opponents off guard and attracting journalists who are always on the lookout for something novel.

Some innovation occurs when protestors realize they can treat a dilemma differently. They often did not realize there *was* a dilemma. One of the great moments of modern protest came on April 30, 1977, when 14 women whose children had been "disappeared" by Argentina's military regime realized that obeying the laws, patiently asking officials for information, was not their only option. They sat down in the Plaza de Mayo in Buenos Aires, a switch from nice to naughty that was a sudden departure for these apolitical housewives whose grief was so devastating that they had nothing left to lose. (It was naughty only in the sense that their repressive government disapproved of it; in many countries it would be accepted as a mainstream tactic.)

The innovation dilemma that we saw with cultural meanings applies as well to tactics. Doing something new may surprise opponents and the media, but it may also unsettle your own team, who lack familiarity and skills to pull off the new tactic. If it is not done well, the result may be worse than not doing anything at all. Likely outcomes are polarized between very good and very bad. Adopting a new tactic is like entering a new arena, always a risky choice. Every new tactic or new arena carries uncertainties, as no player has complete control over how things will proceed. And if things go badly enough in a new engagement, the player who started it all may end up worse off than before.

Bureaucratization curtails innovation because it consists of repeated routines, directing resources and people to familiar operations with predictable results. This predictability is the strength of bureaucracy, but creativity and surprise are the casualties. Because formal organizations are rarely good at innovation, organizations are more likely to die than to adjust if circumstances change. Sometimes leaders can transform the organizations they lead; one definition of charisma is that the leader can command new ways of doing things, breaking free from bureaucratic rigidity. The new tactics can be revolutionary or disastrous, but at least they are new. This is the organization dilemma again: rules make actions predictable, but also inflexible.

Technologies have much the same quality as bureaucracies: they are designed to do one thing well, without a lot of debate. Bullhorns amplify our voices, tear gas irritates human eyes. A given input is supposed to lead to a predictable output. And yet both bureaucracies and technologies can sometimes be adapted to new uses as well.

Internal democracy

If the organization dilemma is about how many formal rules to have, the pyramid dilemma is about how much hierarchy. Rules can be designed to favor flatness or hierarchy. Hierarchy, in turn, can arise from organizations with a lot of rules or very few rules. Ironically, steep pyramids often subvert the formal rules, when leaders who have grown powerful use those rules for their own purposes.

Since the 1960s, most left-leaning protest groups have favored flat pyramids, which is to say, internal democracy in their decision-making. This is often called participatory democracy to distinguish it from representative democracy, where we vote for others who will make decisions on our behalf. In many cases a concern with internal democracy becomes a goal as important as external efficacy. It is seen as **prefigurative**, a version of the kind of equal, democratic world that protestors are hoping to create (Breines 1982). The process of decision-making, with full respect for all participants, becomes more important than the decisions or actions that result. This Janus dilemma led to a cleavage in the global justice movement between those who made process a priority and those (mostly from leftist parties and unions, also known as the "hard left") who cared more about the thrust of the decisions made (Maeckelbergh 2009). To hard-left critics, the general assemblies felt self-indulgent.

Participatory democracy takes a lot of time, or, as one protestor put it in the 1960s, "freedom is an endless meeting" (Polletta 2002). The global justice movement was structured in part by world social forums, regional social forums, and national forums, all of which demanded immense preparation and travel time on top of the days spent at the meetings themselves. For every forum there were dozens or hundreds of preparatory meetings.

This time commitment has its good and bad sides. Debating the issues of the day is exciting for many, especially for newcomers to protest who have not necessarily thought about these issues before. This is how we develop our gut feelings into articulate ideologies, an exciting process. But for those who have already been in many protest groups, the long discussions can feel tedious, especially when doubled in length by the people's mic (although repeating the words yourself, all in unison, can feel good). Some decisions – how to transport laundry to the cleaners – are less weighty than others, but can occupy as much time.

Deciding

Forums and assemblies are small (or not-so-small) experiments in communication. Today's fashion is to discourage the emergence of leaders who might dominate discussions, and the only formal positions are facilitators and other helpers. But this does not prevent informal leaders from emerging, or even dominating (Freeman 1972). Rhetorically, some speakers have more credibility than others. This may be due to their experience and knowledge, such as legal or technical experts or those who have participated for a long time, or it may be due to personal traits such as gender or race. The global justice movement, like many recent egalitarian movements, had a hard time distinguishing reasonable and unreasonable bases for credibility, especially since many participants rejected expert knowledge as part of the authority problem rather than seeing it as part of the democratic solution (Pleyers 2010).

Are meetings fun? Sometimes. When they address profound moral questions that you care about, they can be a deeply satisfying moral experience. They can also arouse curiosity because you don't know the outcomes, and you may enjoy observing the ins and outs that discussions take. Like all arenas, meetings are subject to rules and expectations laid down in advance, and yet the outcomes are never fully predictable. You may just appreciate a good turn of phrase, a theatrical presentation, or a snide joke. A lot happens at meetings off the stage, too. You can ogle, flirt, seduce, or come away with a date. If meetings were always boring, there would be no social movements. Meetings are how collective work is accomplished and individual tasks are assigned. When Naomi Gerstel gave me comments on a draft of this book, she wrote in the margin: "You know you have been to a meeting when you leave with more work to do."

Only the smallest protest groups can remain truly flat pyramids, and even then they are more likely to pretend (and desire) to have no leaders or hierarchy than to actually achieve this. But as soon as they grow too large for all the members to gather in one room and engage each other, they need some structure to aggregate preferences, make decisions, and get work done. This is especially true if a group tries to incorporate different locations, as not everyone can travel to big conferences. The World Social Forum might have attracted tens of thousands of activists (peaking around 150,000 in 2005), but that still left hundreds of thousands back home.

Specialists

One threat to democratic consensus is that some people know more than others. There are experts for any given tactic or kind of knowledge, to whom others may (or may not) defer. They may be legally recognized professionals with extensive training, knowledgeable and experienced participants, or whizzes with some technology. Specialists usually come to expect some deference, or at least credibility, based on their knowledge. Needless to say, expert knowledge and democratic processes are often at odds, based on different sources of authority (Pleyers 2010).

In defining the problems they hope to solve, movements obviously rely on those with knowledge about specialized fields. The antinuclear movements of the 1970s and 1980s sent engineers to public hearings to demonstrate the dangers of nuclear power. Psychologists described the pathologies of wife-beaters in order to challenge police policies and encourage the construction of shelters for battered wives. The global justice movement had economists who could trace the impact of neoliberal policies on growth and inequality, sociologists who could describe their impact on children and the poor. These experts were often doing blame work: demonstrating that markets could be constrained, that policy choices affected outcomes.

There are also experts in tactics, and some tactics can only be carried out by experts. A great deal of the legal system is open only to those familiar with the arcane rules of legal procedures, that is, lawyers. **Cause lawyers** use the law to advance the goals of a social movement, whether suing on behalf of a group or pursuing legal decisions that will change existing laws (Sarat and Scheingold 1998). In the US, Supreme Court decisions are often thought to propel social change, although their primary effects are usually symbolic, such as inspiring a backlash and public controversy. In many cases, protestors try to show that the law promises more justice than it delivers, and often seek trials as a public arena for demonstrating this. That is the core purpose of most civil disobedience, too, whether or not it leads to arrests and court cases.

In a long tradition of sabotage, carried out secretly by individuals or small groups, **hacktivism** is only available to those with formidable computer skills. Hackers have paralyzed or slowed corporate and government websites, including the CIA and the Vatican, and police have fought back with a number of arrests. Jeremy Hammond and his group, Hack this Site, also hacked the computers of at least one rightwing group, planning to use supporters' credit card information to contribute to left-leaning groups. Hammond, a well-known hacker, has been arrested for other types of protest as well, including burning flags, blocking traffic, and "illegal assembly." Hack this Site is devoted to open access and democracy, but participation requires special skills.

Greenpeace, the venerable environmental giant, is also centered on experts, based on the expensive equipment, especially ships, that they use to interfere with nuclear navies, whaling operations, and illegal fishing, in addition to publicity stunts like placing large signs on nuclear reactors and corporate buildings. Its activists are moral virtuosi whom the rest of us can only applaud and admire. And fund: it is no accident that Greenpeace is structured to solicit contributions from large numbers of people to support a small band of pugnacious specialists.

We see a continuum here, from single, highly skilled individuals acting on their own to elaborate teams like a law firm or a Greenpeace ship, which need extensive financial backing.

Factions

All groups experience disagreements from time to time. Sometimes these are a healthy way for the group to explore alternatives, pushing it to think more carefully about its options, articulate its goals, and defend its positions. In other cases the conflict destroys the group. In still others, the group remains together but factions form who disagree again and again, often building up mistrust and dislike, even hatred, for each other.

We tend to like people who agree with us, and to agree with people we like. As a result, clusters of like-minded people emerge in all decision-making arenas. These factions may develop into formal political parties in electoral systems, but social movements are rarely so established as to have formal divisions like that. They certainly have informal ones, however. Factions form around ideological or strategic disagreements, although they also arise out of emotional bonds, some of which may have existed before the group even formed. We feel more comfortable with people who are like us in some way, and certainly with people we already know and like. Friends and acquaintances usually cluster together, as do people from similar class or racial-ethnic backgrounds, who have different ways of talking politically (Leondar-Wright 2014). Gender seems to have an especially strong influence, as women and men are socialized to have different sensibilities, and even today spend much of their time in sex-segregated activities.

Factions not only embrace conflicting goals or means, they come to be symbols of them too. Choices about what to do become choices about "who we are." In the US civil rights movement, consensus and participatory democracy came to be associated with white participants, especially college students who came for Freedom Summer in 1964 and stayed (Polletta 2002). Arguing for tighter structure and against consensus was a way for local black activists to push whites out of their organization. In the global justice movement, horizontalism was similarly understood as a critique of the "organized left" of parties and unions. Participants cared about the tactics, but also about who was associated with those tactics. Verticalist factions sometimes reacted against participatory democracy in the global justice movement by preparing their speakers and crafting their positions beforehand and by packing the speakers' list – something made easier by the fact that the verticalists already agreed upon ideology and tactics.

Factional disputes come about partly from the extension dilemma: extending your movement to include many different perspectives increases its size but also its diversity, running the risk of internal disputes that can interfere with external programs of action. Strategic dilemmas impose choices, around which conflict frequently arises. Different sides want to pursue different solutions to the dilemma, depending partly on their tastes in tactics. The battles and mistrust between the horizontal and the organized left in the global justice movement surfaced in one decision after another.

Generations are also the basis for many disagreements. I don't necessarily mean parents and children, an age difference of 20 or 30 years, although that almost inevitably brings disagreements too. Generations in a protest group can be much finer, as a difference of just a year or two when someone joins can affect their tastes in tactics, their collective identities, and their political goals. In most cases, an event changes the mood, hopes, and tactics of movement recruits: those joining the global justice movement after Seattle in 1999 had a different, often more naughty, vision of the movement (and for the movement) than those who had joined before.

In both kinds of generational divides, the younger recruits are often responding to two things: the real-world problem that is the focus of the movement, and the way in which the older generation of protestors has tried to deal with it. Often, they are upset about both. A newer cohort may have more radical tastes in tactics, and chafe at existing movement leaders' safer repertories. They may be just as angry at the protest leaders – for selling out perhaps – as they are at the movement's target. Since political engagements evolve rapidly, this summer's recruits may see the situation very differently from last summer's (Whittier 1995).

It is dynamics like these, in which factions of protestors react to each other as well as to external players, that sometimes lead to **radical flanks**, blocs that pride themselves on pursuing more aggressive tactics than other groups in a movement. Radical wings can have a variety of impacts, both good and bad, on a movement (Haines 1988). They tend to be threatening or colorful enough to attract media attention, but they heighten the risks of the media dilemma, in that the media do not necessarily portray the movement as it wants to be depicted. Journalists report on the wacky radicals rather than on the issues they raise. It is not just reporters who respond to radicals: your opponents try to discredit you with character work aimed at portraying your entire movement as too radical, dangerous, or misguided.

By definition, radicals push the naughty or nice dilemma in the naughty direction. A radical flank may frighten authorities into concessions, or into recognizing moderates as suitable (or at least preferable) negotiating partners. As with any aggressive, unpopular tactics, there is a greater chance of repression. The risks increase. There are also internal effects of radical flanks: those who admire strong tactics are energized, while those who dislike them are alienated.

Factions often work out their differences or agree to disagree, but they sometimes split into two groups. *Schisms* of this kind are not always destructive; they allow a variety of different groups to work more or less independently toward the same or related ends. Because they pursue different tactics, they are more likely to hit on some that are successful. Many strategic dilemmas are resolved in this way. For example the media dilemma: once radicals attract the attention of journalists, more moderate groups can then articulate the issues in a form suitable for mass consumption (Gamson and Wolfsfeld 1993: 121).

Depending on how nasty the fight was, however, former allies may devote more time to criticizing each other than to battling common enemies, a tendency especially of Marxist sects, superbly mocked in Monty Python's *Life of Brian*, when the People's Front of Judea sneers at the nearby Judean People's Front. Such infighting is not always a joke: in 1930s Germany, communists attacked socialists in the streets at the same time that the Nazis were gaining the strength to seize power and outlaw them both.

Some groups and even entire movements grow more radical over time, others less so. With formal organizations and stable funding, groups tend to grow complacent and moderate. For this reason, newcomers often reject existing groups and form new, more radical, ones. New recruits may bring different tastes in tactics, but they may also pride themselves on an identity as "radicals," different from prior cohorts of protestors. Some Occupiers for example were critical of the global justice movement for what they saw as its emphasis on talk rather than direct action.

Protest groups can also radicalize through their own experiences, especially when the channels for complaints are blocked or when authorities spurn them. They then develop grievances about procedures, which can be especially provoking because they mean democracy has failed.

Strategic dilemmas and decisions

All strategic players face tradeoffs or dilemmas, and their emotional and cognitive visions show why they ignore some but wrestle intently with others. Some tradeoffs are ignored because one option is simply not available: a tiny group that has no prospects of expanding does not need to wrestle with the extension or the organization dilemma. The history of a group may also steer it away from some dilemmas: if it had a bitter fight over extension, it may avoid this topic for a long time, or the battle may have led those on one side of the dilemma to split and form their own group. In other cases, tastes in tactics prevent discussions of many alternatives, and there are always instances when a group simply does not think of doing anything differently thanks to its cultural blinders. Most tradeoffs never make their way into consciousness to become acknowledged dilemmas.

A number of dilemmas have to do with risk-taking, such as naughty or nice and the innovation dilemma, pitting safe against risky options. Others deal with tradeoffs between short-run and long-run goals. The organization dilemma is one of these: to build an organization, you invest time and effort now in the hopes that it will pay off later thanks to the enduring bureaucracy you have constructed. But it may be the short run where the biggest gains can occur: the wildcat strike, the riot, the unexpected and spontaneous tactic. And for many movements there simply *is* no long run without short-run victories. More generally, short- and long-run goals conflict simply because of limited time and energy.

Decisions about organizational structures and routines are also decisions about tactics, since who is involved and what they do are always entwined. Political scientist Jane Mansbridge (1986) offers an example from the movement for the Equal Rights Amendment (ERA) in the United States, aimed at getting two-thirds of state legislatures to ratify the proposed amendment. The movement, with little coordinated structure and few rules, relied primarily on volunteer staff and self-selected advocates, especially feminist law professors who were often quite radical for the time. There was no central control over what these spokespeople said in interviews or opinion pieces (blogs had not been invented). Their vision was that the ERA would allow women to be combat soldiers, and some even insisted that it also implied coed toilets – exactly the implications that the amendment's opponents were using against it. Here, the volunteer radical flank was running the show, and in the case that Mansbridge studied – the crucial state of Illinois – this brought defeat for the ERA.

Because of rational choice theories, scholars tend to think of decision-making as a matter of rational calculation, when everyone sits down in a room and debates the best options. They do meet and discuss, but they bring emotions with them. They are more likely to agree with people they like and trust, more likely to reject what is said by someone who annoys them. If they are in a good mood, they are more likely to support expansive tactics, take greater risks, and expect things to work out. They may feel a wave of disgust over certain tactics, or instead a proud swelling over the moral power of tactics that embody their ideals. They may harbor anger because their own proposal was rejected last time, and refuse to support anything else. And of course in these settings, leaders bring out feelings of admiration, love, envy, bitterness, and more.

There are many ways to make decisions. Certain individuals or committees can be charged with making proposals; that role may fall exclusively to a group's leaders. There may be open meetings to generate ideas, or at least to make members feel that the group is open to everyone's suggestions. There may be a number of planning meetings to set the rules for more formal meetings. Once ideas are generated they may be discussed – or not. And the final choice may be taken through a vote of all those involved, a small group or a single leader, or through efforts to find a consensus.

For many recent groups, votes are a sign of a failure to reach the consensus required of true democracy.

How a group handles a choice depends on the collected individuals, what they know, how they feel, what resources they can marshal. Diverse backgrounds can often help by generating diverse suggestions (Ganz 2000). Individuals learn as they move from one group to another, one situation to the next. In any given situation, they think of past experiences in similar settings, not necessarily explicitly but often implicitly, intuitively sensing what can possibly happen, what other players are likely to feel and do. What looks like mysterious intuition is actually a well-trained ability to think fast, to think unconsciously.

Most of all, strategic action consists of reacting to what other players do, whether those players are friends or foes, or your own fellow members. Because there are usually a lot of players, and it is impossible to predict perfectly what they will do, advance plans rarely work out. The police mass in one street, demonstrators head down another. Reporters are losing interest? Do something they haven't seen before. Often, innovations arise from the inevitable improvisation of strategic battles.

* * *

We have viewed social movements as arenas in this chapter, looking inside them to see how they make decisions, or in some cases avoid decisions. We have seen several factors that shape these processes. Some groups tend to rely on bureaucratic mechanisms, while others try to retain flexibility and creativity. Some are more loyal to internal democracy, seeing this not only as an end in itself but also as the way to preserve a flexible openness to strategic possibilities. In contrast, some activities require special skills that give a small number of people considerable authority. The factions that inevitably form can destroy a movement, split it into several parts, or push it in more radical directions. All these processes revolve around strategic tradeoffs, some of which are taken on as explicit dilemmas for decision-making.

A few protest groups make consistently good decisions, some make poor ones; most make both good and bad choices. Obviously, good decisions are those more likely to advance the movement's cause. But even the best decisions do not guarantee victory for a movement. After all, opponents are making their own decisions, deploying their own strategies, monitoring what the movement is doing, and trying to block it. In most cases, they have greater resources and special access to decision-making arenas. Protestors can sometimes overcome their disadvantages with clever strategies, but not always. Strategic engagements always hold uncertainty.

7

Engaging Other Players

The Egyptian Revolution

No one expected Egypt's uprising in January 2011. There had been disgust, frustration, and resignation over Mubarak's cronyist regime for decades, and efforts to mobilize around two grisly killings by Alexandria's police in 2010 had failed despite the extensive use of Facebook. People were shocked but remained cynical – although millions soon embraced Khaled Said, one of the Alexandria victims, as a symbol of regime violence. The Facebook group "We are all Khaled Said" grew to half a million members.

Then a fruit vendor named Mohamed Bouazizi set himself on fire in Tunisia in December 2010, and after a month of protests – on January 14 – Tunisia's dictator panicked and fled the country. Suddenly, there was hope in Egypt to go along with the indignation, a moral battery. What could happen in Tunisia could happen in Egypt.

Demonstrations against police brutality, held mischievously on National Police Day, January 25, 2011, drew tens of thousands of Cairo protestors, who managed to coordinate their marches partly via cellphones and social media. At first they demanded term limits on the president, not his resignation. Several days later, the government shut down cellphone and internet access for most Egyptians, but old-fashioned face-to-face networks plugged the gap: the 28th was a Friday, when mosques filled with the faithful.

Buoyed by the feeling of solidarity that religious rituals provide, by the feeling that God was on their side, hundreds of thousands took to the streets after prayers. Two anxious weeks followed: some concessions from Mubarak, attacks on demonstrators by armed thugs, and the army's crucial decision not to intervene. Protest against police violence, met with brutal intransigence, escalated into demands for the regime's end. A protest movement developed into a revolutionary movement.

The giant tent camp in Tahrir Square grew steadily. Despite the dangers, people were on holiday, hopeful of big changes and thus in a good mood, another joyous bivouac. Each victory, small or large, amplified the emotional energy of that mood. Tahrir was a sea of signs, mostly urging Mubarak to go ("I wash my hands of you until the day of judgment") or simply expressing feelings ("People hate you"). Some apologized for not acting sooner ("Forgive me Lord, I was afraid and silent"). A group of four brothers, whose two other brothers had been killed, strikingly taped their mouths shut ("No talk until he leaves") (Khalil 2011).

With Tahrir's exhilaration as background, each attack – verbal or physical – by Mubarak's thugs and spokespersons created more indignation than fear. Or rather, indignation was a good way to transform the negative mood of anxiety into a positive mood. Tahrir Square became a carnival, a moment of madness, a kind of dream. Throughout the city people talked with their neighbors, formed neighborhood watches, helped strangers who had been tear-gassed. The outrage peaked on February 10, when Mubarak went on television and – instead of the expected resignation – gave a meandering but defiant speech. The next day, another Friday, the crowds swelled enormously. Mubarak resigned that evening.

The overthrow of a dictator is the end of one story but the beginning of another, a shift from the arena of the street to many others, often hidden from view. Most revolutions bring together a broad coalition that shares only its indignation against the old regime (one no, many yeses, to borrow from the global justice movement), but once that lightning rod for hatred and defiance is removed, then the coalition splits into its component, and competing, players.

A military council took power after Mubarak's resignation,

pledging to step down after a constitutional referendum and elections. Protests continued over some of the Supreme Council's decisions, and groups broke into the offices of the secret police to search their files, unsurprisingly turning up evidence of mass surveillance under Mubarak. After the new constitution was approved, the council proved willing to detain and prosecute former Mubarak officials, but it also imposed heavy fines for protest activities, thereby inspiring more protest. For months, protestors returned to the streets, especially on Fridays, with numbers in the hundreds of thousands. They often clashed with police, and dozens were killed.

In November 2011, with protests growing, the Council apologized for the deaths of protestors and appointed a civilian prime minister, partly because of pressure by the US government. In April 2012, after parliamentary, but before presidential, elections, a high administrative court entered the fray, disbanding the new assembly charged with drafting another constitution. In June, Egypt's Supreme Court declared the parliamentary elections invalid, and the armed forces again took control. The revolution faltered.

The Muslim Brotherhood's extensive networks were easily transformed into a political party, and its candidate Mohamed Morsi was elected president on June 24, 2012. Initially, he showed strategic acumen, reinstating the parliament that the courts had annulled and cleverly promoting the two strongest military leaders on the Council to be his personal advisors, removing them (and several others) from the key player, the army.

In November, Morsi took another step, purporting to protect the work of the constitutional assembly but giving himself whatever powers he needed to protect the revolution – his revolution. Protestors returned to the streets, especially secular demonstrators who feared the Muslim Brotherhood. Morsi may have run afoul of the innovation dilemma, pushing too many changes too fast – but also passing laws that gave him powers far beyond those necessary to protect the revolution. He failed to make alliances with liberal parties, deepening their mistrust rather than redressing it. He began to look too strong, as well as incompetent in managing the economy.

Millions took to the streets on June 30, 2013, with a variety of economic and political grievances but also aiming to enjoy the festival, in what may have been the largest single demonstration ever. They welcomed an army coup that removed Morsi from office on July 3. The army imprisoned hundreds of Brotherhood leaders and excluded the party from any positions in the new government. The Obama administration protested by withholding military jets it had promised, but soon accepted the new situation by refusing to condemn it as a coup. In several incidents, hundreds of pro-Brotherhood demonstrators were injured and killed.

Egypt's revolution unfolded over several years, a contest among parties, politicians, the army, high judges, unions, and between Islamist and non-Islamist protest movements (once revolutionary allies). In new and old arenas, players struggled for power, including the power to shape the arenas. As a spokesman for the Brotherhood said in June 2012: "It is a chessboard. They made a move and we made a move." And many more moves. By the start of 2014, however, the army had tightened its control, to the extent of declaring the Muslim Brotherhood a terrorist group.

A **revolution** is a special kind of outcome, in which a new political regime is established, with changes in the structure of government and not merely – as with normal elections – changes in the parties in power. Many revolutionary movements fail to achieve a revolution. Revolutions are rare, but we study and sometimes admire them because they are so important in world history. The new regimes, especially at first, are usually improvements over what they replace. Because revolutions inspire people, they leave behind moral visions and ideals as well as new government bureaucracies.

The study of revolutions and the study of other social movements have been oddly distant for many years, in part because revolutions are chains of so many distinct phases and processes, involving different sets of players in different phases. But revolutions are exemplary in one way: they show that politics is an interaction among multiple players, spilling across many arenas, over extended periods of time. Specifying those players, arenas, and interactions is key to explaining both protest and revolutions.

Ultimately, protestors want to change the world around them, and their relative success depends on their ability to coerce, persuade, or buy off other players, who may be sympathetic, hostile, or neutral, but all of whom have tactics and goals of their own. We can view them through the same interpretive lens we have used for protest groups: asking what they want, how they see the world, what dilemmas they face, what resources and routines they rely on, who their allies and rivals are. Only then can we understand how they interact with protestors to produce wins, losses, and other impacts of protest.

The forces of order

Among the many players that form the state, protestors interact most regularly with the *police* and related "forces of order" such as soldiers, paid bullies, riot police, traffic police, spies, and private security services like embassy guards or the Pinkerton Detective Agency. In all nations, police forces monitor and spy on protest groups, sometimes quite extensively. (At the height of the Red Scare in the US in the 1950s, it is estimated, one-third of the members of the Communist Party were FBI agents, who also seem to have been the backbone of the postwar Ku Klux Klan.) In Cairo, hundreds of police were deployed at each of the 20 rallying points advertised on Facebook for January 25, 2011, blocking many marches, and the most successful march started at a site intentionally kept secret and off Facebook.

Police face their own choices of whether to be naughty or nice, and countries differ enormously in how well police treat demonstrations. In the world's more tolerant nations, protest organizers expect to negotiate a range of issues with the police in advance, such as where they will march, how many will be arrested, and what other activities will be permitted. In less tolerant countries, they expect to be harassed, beaten, arrested, and sometimes killed for their activities.

At one time, police had a free hand everywhere, and torture and execution were common policing tools. Intense pain crowds out other goals, and any future plans, so that its victim will often do anything to stop it, including revealing secret information about comrades and clandestine activities. The victims with the strongest ideologies and collective identities seem to withstand the pain longer, so deep are their loyalties to others, so strong their sense of purpose.

Short of torture, repressive regimes have other means of intimidation. In Egypt, armored vehicles sped through the streets, sometimes hitting pedestrians; hundreds of officers marched or ran, in a thuggish military cadence, and – most desperately – fired into the crowds that constantly encircled them. Under both Mubarak and Morsi, police sprayed protestors with water cannons, beat them, tear-gassed and sometimes shot them. Most of all, commanders tried to ensure that the police outnumbered protestors at all times, a lesson applied these days in New York as well as in Cairo. When they feel strong, security forces sometimes show a human face, talking with demonstrators, smiling, even singing along. Police turn out to be human, protestors sometimes remark. When they feel threatened, however, the police still resort to violence.

In Cairo in 2011, the numbers shifted in favor of the demonstrators. Instead of massed police surrounding demonstrators, wave upon wave of protestors arrived from various quarters and surrounded the police, who were terrified as they found themselves outnumbered. And rightly so: police cars were stopped and overturned; officers spraying fire hoses were pulled off their trucks; black riot helmets were flying through the air during brawls. The police may have been bruised but they were not killed, since they, rather than the protestors, were the ones with the guns. In contrast to the police, Egypt's army were in tanks, so they were not likely to feel threatened. This helped them remain calm, waiting for strategic decisions taken by their commanders, who in turn were interacting with other players such as their financial patrons in Washington.

Until the 1970s, police in most western democracies treated most demonstrators in the same way, as criminals who had to be subdued, and they would deploy more and more force until crowds dispersed or were arrested. But the police learned – slowly and incompletely – that brutality tends to make protestors angrier, so that violence escalates. Public attitudes toward demonstrators become more sympathetic, and police usually conformed, especially when cellphone video capacities vastly increased the chances that a brutal act would make the evening news or go viral on the internet. Police became more professional, tolerating more protest activities, negotiating with protest leaders beforehand, preventing trespassing and violence rather than waiting for it, trying to avoid injuries on both sides, and following the laws rather than seeing themselves as above the law (della Porta and Reiter 1998).

But after the Seattle protests in 1999, and especially with the widespread panic following 9/11, police became more aggressive again. They began to fence off restricted areas, to make pre-emptive arrests of protest leaders, and to corral demonstrators into restricted, uncomfortable side streets and barricaded pens. Under cover of new antiterrorist legislation, and with increased technological powers, US police forces increased their surveillance of protestors. They did their own far-fetched character work to depict a variety of peaceful protestors as terrorists, dangerous "villains" rather than legitimate political players, against whom they needed vast government funding.

In grappling with the naughty or nice dilemma, police respond in part to the desires of the politicians and bureaucrats who control their budgets. Some politicians wish to look progressive and tolerant of protest. Others want to prove they are tough, and allow the police more leeway in dealing with protest. In those cases police corral demonstrators, deal roughly with them, detain large numbers, and prosecute those arrested. (They also try to influence politicians' preferences so that they do not interfere with the police.) They are strategic players like any other.

Armies have different goals from those of the police. They are trained in heavy weapons intended to fight wars against other armies, not to put down protest in their own nations, something that most soldiers dislike doing. Some armies contain draftees who may prove sympathetic to dissent, as well. Even with purely professional armies, there is a pronounced distance between the

commanders at the top and the grunts at the bottom, with different perspectives and feelings about the world, so that cleavages
can form.

The Egyptian army received billions of dollars in aid, as well as
training, from the US, which therefore had some influence over
the army's decisions. In contrast to previous presidents, who had
supported a long string of nasty dictators around the world, the
Obama administration came to support the protestors in Tahrir
Square. The army had also grown distant from Mubarak, who,
although once a general, had increasingly concentrated on enrich-
ing his own family instead of the army. The Egyptian army's
choices were crucial to the unfolding outcomes all along.

Because both armies and police sometimes sympathize with
moral protest, dictators usually form *special units* of guards or
secret police, with extra privileges or ethnic ties to the leader.
Their job is to protect the dictator at all costs. They are usually the
last to defect in a revolution. Many corrupt regimes also secretly
hire *criminals* to perform the nastiest jobs, which professional
police or military will not do, a kind of radical flank of individuals who can attack protestors but are not wearing uniforms. The
regime can deny any connection, even claiming that these are
outraged citizens acting on their own. (In some cases they may
actually be citizen vigilantes without ties to the government, but
the protestors have an interest in portraying them as paid goons
rather than outraged citizens with their own, opposed, moral
visions.) There are private police forces too, operating outside
most laws. The notorious Pinkerton Detective Agency employed
spies and *agents provocateurs* as well as forming small armies who
in many cases fired upon unarmed strikers, doing serious damage
to the American labor movement in its early decades. (The agency
still exists.)

Both public and private police send spies and provocateurs to
disrupt protest organizations in stealthy ways. They try to make
group members suspect one another, for instance by sending
anonymous letters accusing them of corruption or of spying for
the police. They send information and accusations to protestors'
employers, or, if they are students, to their schools and universities.

150

They supply embarrassing information, often fraudulent, to journalists, and try to make different groups wary of each other. They
try to make protest groups appear more radical – or just weirder –
than they are, like the man at an Occupy rally with a sign saying,
"Google: Zionists Control Wall Street." (Occupiers responded by
following him around Zuccotti Park with their own signs saying,
"Who pays this guy? He doesn't speak for me or OWS!")

Judicial arenas

Arrests place protestors in another set of arenas, the courts. Legal
courts are now universal, although with varying degrees of inde-
pendence from the rest of the state, ranging from being proudly
autonomous, as in South Africa, to being abjectly servile, as under
most dictators. Laws are intended to define and enforce the norms
of legitimate and illegitimate political action, to embody the meanings and morals of a territorial unit, and so they are constant
targets for protestors as well as tools for their opponents.

Some trials become symbols of a cause to broad audiences,
who follow the proceedings intently. **Symbolic trials** may arise
accidentally, or the government may intend to have show trials to
demonstrate the limits of its tolerance. In some cases protestors
themselves hope that a large trial will be a new arena through
which they can convey their messages to new audiences, or prove
their points about the repressive impulses of the state. With class
action suits, plaintiffs hope to change policies and awareness, like
the *Dukes v. Walmart* suit that proposed to represent no fewer
than 1.6 million American women who had worked for the retail
behemoth. That is much more than symbolic.

Courtrooms offer moving character dramas by stripping down
contestation to a handful of players and attempting to make clear
decisions about victims and villains. A protestor who has broken
the law: is she a hero, as her comrades believe, or is she a villain,
even a common criminal?

Courts contain several official players. In some countries *judges*
are thought to preside over (officially) neutral arenas in which

prosecutors or plaintiffs battle against defendants, while in other nations judges are an investigating arm of the state. Upholding the law according to proper procedures is the core professional message that *lawyers* receive in their training, although judges at higher levels also assume responsibility for interpreting the law as well. (All laws are applied through interpretation, in fact, but this is not always admitted.) *Public prosecutors* must decide whether to bring a protestor to trial, torn between their goal of repressing unlawful activities and their fear that the trial will simply bring more publicity and sympathy to the cause.

In common-law systems, *jurors* are another player; they may have greater sympathies for protestors than prosecutors realize, imposing dilemmas on the latter. Juries often refuse to deliver the harsh verdicts that prosecutors request. In recent years British juries have acquitted activists who, claiming "necessity" defenses in the face of immediate threats, had damaged fields of genetically modified crops, the offices of weapons contractors, and coal-fired power plants (Doherty and Hayes 2014).

High courts such as the US Supreme Court are more player than arena in deciding which decisions and policies to review. In Egypt, top courts issued several rulings in spring 2012 that affected the unfolding revolution: they suspended the constitutional assembly in April, struck down a law banning former Mubarak politicians from running for office in June, dissolved the new parliament, and yet also revoked a decree giving military police the power to arrest civilians. Most of these actions blunted the revolution, leading most of the public to see the court as a (reactionary) political player rather than a neutral arena, but the revocation of the pro-military decree restored a bit of courtly credibility. High court appointees retained some loyalty to Mubarak that rank-and-file lawyers – many of whom joined the 2011 protests – did not share.

Politicians and journalists

Political parties and the *legislators* who belong to them are the ultimate target for many social movements, the source of new laws and policies that can fulfill protestors' goals. Foremost, politicians want to be re-elected, and parties also want to get their members into office and keep them there. Public opinion obviously drives their choices, but they pay special attention to their own supporters (especially financial supporters) and to voters on the margin between two parties, voters whom they might win over with the right policies but lose with the wrong ones.

Policies are not everything, and politicians make more statements than they do laws. Their words matter, and it is often satisfying for a social movement to be taken seriously enough to be acknowledged at all. Like other strategic players, politicians often send different messages to different audiences: a populist, anti-corporate rhetoric may win votes, even while the same politician works behind the scenes to protect corporate interests, making obscure choices that only paid lobbyists notice. But when protestors win a statement of support they can sometimes transform it into a vote.

Journalists are also key players in contemporary conflicts, we have seen, not only because they shape public opinion but because they also influence the perceptions of protestors and politicians about their *own* situations. Although protestors have their own criticisms of media bias, and large movements have alternative media, movements often turn to mainstream media to assess government intentions and the general mood of the population. Politicians are influenced by journalistic representations of public opinion; they hesitate to get too far out of line on salient issues.

Those who create the news, whether on websites, newspapers, radio, or television, have their own goals and methods. Journalists are usually paid to cover particular beats, typically structured around government arenas like courts or legislatures; they must meet deadlines, and please editors and owners. They try to deliver stories that will attract audiences, which often means stories of individuals, with some suspense, about actions rather than ongoing states of things, and especially novel and photogenic forms of action. Only some protests are deemed "newsworthy" (Gitlin 1980). And only some protestors: while government officials are regularly granted the status of legitimate news sources to be interviewed, protestors rarely are. They are covered more for their actions than for their opinions, especially actions that threaten to break the law. Editors often assign protests to the police beat, framing demonstrators as potential lawbreakers.

Protest groups work hard to break this **news barrier,** holding mock interviews with each other, designing slick press releases, inventing soundbites and good visuals. Ironically, journalists often dismiss such activities as inauthentic "press stunts" when protestors appear to be working too hard to attract journalists (Sobieraj 2011). Like all good performances, demonstrations must appear spontaneous; the best acting does not feel like acting. (Sociologist Arlie Hochschild distinguishes *surface acting,* when you put on the right expressions and gestures, from *deep acting,* when you actually feel what you are supposed to be expressing.) It should not appear as if you have practiced your performance.

Despite professional norms embracing objectivity, hard to follow under the best of circumstances, journalists sometimes become more active players. This may be nothing more than helping to bring attention to a social problem through coverage and editorials, usually problems that the middle class can condemn, such as obesity, smoking, or in some cases excessive pay for corporate executives. Sometimes journalists are forced to take sides, especially when government officials or the police attack them for – in the journalists' eyes – doing their job. Mubarak officials accused foreign journalists of being Israeli agents, and they arrested some Al Jazeera reporters. Pro-Mubarak thugs sacked Al Jazeera's Cairo office. Al Jazeera returned the favor by pointing out the lies perpetrated by official television, boosting the network's standing with protestors, who at one point on February 6, 2011 chanted "Long Live Al Jazeera!"

The internet has decentralized the flow of information across worldwide networks, and people get news from each other as well as from journalists. Regimes still try to control these sources, since there are central nodes in this worldwide network, service providers whose electricity and offices can be shut down. This is not as easy as flipping a switch. The Mubarak regime tried this in the early days of Egypt's 2011 revolution. First they blocked text messages. Then they asked the four main internet service providers to disconnect their routers. Two days later they asked another service provider, Noor Data Services, to disconnect, even though transactions on Cairo's stock exchange were stopped as a result. The blackout was not total, as small providers, especially at universities, continued to operate, and a few Egyptians still had dial-up modems and fax machines they could use (Castells 2012).

Hackers and activists around the world responded to the shutdown by reconfiguring their own systems to channel information to and from Egypt. Twitter quickly developed new procedures to convert voice messages into tweets, and new hash tags to distribute them. Hackers with Telecomix figured out how to convert voice messages to texts and to send them to every fax machine operating in Egypt. Old-fashioned telephone lines substituted for the internet in this and other ways. (The brief internet shutdown cost the Egyptian economy almost $100 million.)

Potential allies

Intellectuals, including academics, novelists, artists, and others who think and create for a living and have found some public audience for their products, frequently see their exertions as a kind of politics, and they also – like everyone else – on occasion become part of a social movement. When they join a movement, or at least are sympathetic to it, they can concentrate on presenting the movement's hopes and ideology, in contrast to journalists who have many other goals. We saw that books, music, and other creative products can inspire and "certify" a social movement to members themselves as well as to outsiders. A special kind of *organic intellectual* grows from within the movement, crafting the arguments, brochures, and magazines that help a movement articulate its values and debate its tactics. Their audience is usually the movement itself, although they can be drafted as spokespeople for the media and other audiences.

Celebrities are similar to intellectuals in having their own audiences, who follow what they do, say, and wear. They are often drawn to social movements, speaking out about an issue, raising funds through concerts and appearances, and lending their images to advertisements. Even the best-intentioned public intellectuals and celebrities pose the powerful-allies dilemma for a movement (which organic intellectuals do not): they have their own definition of the cause, their own reputations to worry about, and their own passions.

Bystanders are a loose category of people who watch the action in a political arena without participating themselves. Some bystanders have the potential to turn into players, like politicians who have not yet taken a stand on some controversial matter. Other bystanders might have an indirect effect, like individuals moved to write letters to their member of parliament about some particular issue. Politicians tend to track public opinion, and rarely take positions that are highly unpopular, or at least unpopular with their core voters. Even when bystanders are not likely to influence or become players, it is often satisfying to win them over to your cause, since that reassures you that you are on the side of justice. In many cases we imagine what bystanders are thinking and feeling without actually finding out. They are a symbol of broader audiences.

Other protest groups, in the same or related movements, can be competitors, allies, or both at the same time. You may share a goal with them, such as overthrowing Mubarak, but disagree so much over tactics that it is impossible to work together. Or you may compete with them for attention, members, funds, and control over the definition and outcome of the cause. The young, liberal protestors who belonged to "We are all Khaled Said" were in the streets again chanting similar things about Morsi that they had said about Mubarak, doing battle with their former Islamist allies.

The line between bystanders and other protest groups often blurs, and it is good strategy to try to shift that line. In Egypt, many protests included soccer fans, accustomed to moving in crowds and singing their favorite songs and slogans. Activated by police repression, they gave a festive air to many marches and rallies. But they were also not afraid to mix it up with the police, something they had experience with. Here was bloc recruitment at its best.

When cooperation is possible, *coalitions* allow groups to work together while maintaining their own identities – and always retaining the right to pull out if a coalition moves in a direction antithetical to the group's core identity. Coalitions can be formal or informal, long-lasting or briefly arranged for a specific purpose. Nothing is automatic about alliances: they require extensive persuasion and emotion work, typically on the part of the leaders of the groups involved.

Donors are a special kind of ally, providing useful resources – mostly money, but also advice, offices, places for rallies, and other useful items. *Foundations*, led by the Ford Foundation in the 1960s, have become important sources of seed money for young groups, in many cases ironically using money originally derived from corporate profits to undo some of the harm done by corporate practices. Those who hand out foundation grants have their own moral visions and professional standards, but they must also please their bosses and boards – much like journalists who face their own pressures from above. Most radicals treat the grant officers with suspicion, partly because foundations tend to favor cautious, legal means of action. Regulators might well shut them down if they did not, as elaborate laws govern foundation activities.

International donors pose a special risk, since they have rich-country resources that are very seductive to poor-country protestors, who as a result are often willing to rework their character and identity to fit the donors' preferred ideas about worthy victims (Bob 2005). A year into the Egyptian revolution, the interim government, still dominated by the military, began harassing US-based groups that promoted democratic reforms and participation, perhaps unsure whether expanded participation would suit the military's interests in the long run (probably not).

Protestors want and need different things from different players, crafting their appeals specially for each one. These other players interact with each other at the same time, often to block the actions of social movements. A swarm of different players constantly observe each other, anticipate actions, and craft their own plans of attack. Whether protestors win or lose depends on this buzzing interaction, which spills across diverse arenas.

Arenas of conflict

Varying combinations of these players engage each other in a range of arenas, each with its own rules, positions, and stakes. Protestors promote their goals in several arenas, and often switch between arenas when they see opportunities for progress. They must constantly monitor and interpret what all the players are doing in the relevant (and potentially relevant) arenas. At their most successful, movements actually change the rules of arenas or accept positions within them, making it easier for them to influence future developments.

In addition to courtrooms and legislative battles, common arenas include: public *demonstrations* intended to influence participants, passers-by, the media, and governments; *elections* whose outcomes protestors hope to influence; *debates* over issues of public concern, which unfold through books, editorials, blogs, and other media; public *hearings* at which representatives of protest groups testify; the *walls* of buildings that protestors cover with graffiti or posters; *media events* such as political conventions, coronations, or inaugurations where protestors can be assured of some attention if they disrupt things. Protestors can also seize factories, or boycott stores, banks, suppliers, or elections – turning almost any activity or place into an arena for contestation.

Legal tactics are open to protestors who wish to remain within the law, participating in institutionalized routines such as writing to politicians, bringing lawsuits, or peacefully gathering in public spaces. In many of these activities, protest looks like any other kind of politics, but when it moves outdoors, into the streets and squares, it becomes a classic social movement. Although these used to be labeled as "non-institutional" politics, because they did not involve parties and parliaments, we have seen that outdoor protest is well institutionalized in some nations. In more repressive regimes, there are – by definition – more restrictions. Initially, Egyptian protestors stood five feet apart, in silence, in order to comply with rules against public gatherings.

An action that is legal in one country may be banned in

another, including apparently straightforward activities such as marches and rallies. *Illegal* tactics often challenge the laws that make them illegal, as we saw in the Wilkes agitation in chapter 1. **Civil disobedience** combines coercion and persuasion. Arrests are a token of thoughtful commitment, entailing considerable time, perhaps fines, and the risk of something more serious such as bodily harm, or in some regimes even death. They also make the news.

Other illegal activities may be aimed not at legal questions or persuasion, but at direct harm or retribution against opponents, such as burning down a barn belonging to a nasty landlord or sabotaging a machine in a factory. These entail coercion more than persuasion, and they can harm either property or people.

Arguing for the naughty option of the naughty or nice dilemma, Frances Fox Piven and Richard Cloward (1977) famously argued that poor people, facing elaborate laws intended to control them, only advance their rights and interests when they *disrupt* activities that elites value. The most famous example is the sit-down strikes of the 1930s, when workers occupied assembly lines that were vital to producing General Motors automobiles. Workers held the key to GM's revenues and profits, and after six weeks the world's largest corporation recognized the United Auto Workers as the exclusive bargaining agent for its workers. (The workers were demanding only this simple recognition, nothing more.) Riots, strikes, and other types of occupation are also examples of disruption that attract immediate attention, as do boycotts. For those with few resources, this approach may work best.

In their complementary formulation of the organization dilemma, Piven and Cloward argue that when poor people form organizations, such as unions, to advance their interests, these organizations betray them, because leaders grow more interested in maintaining the organization than in winning victories for its members. Union leaders become fond of their high salaries and travel, begin to play golf with managers, and to see the union's size and strength as their primary concern. Piven and Cloward downplay the other horn of the dilemma: organizations sometimes provide benefits. (If organizations were always bad, there would be no dilemma, and we might wonder why activists were ever fooled into establishing them.)

Even the most oppressed groups, most of the time, avoid pitched confrontations. So what helps them decide to put down the tools of the status quo and to disrupt things instead? In a word, emotions. Anger and indignation must reach a point where people are willing to take great risks for the common good. Often, a moral shock propels them to higher levels of activity and confrontation. This is not an automatic reaction; leaders must use the shock to reinforce existing loyalties and moral emotions, to instill a sense of urgency – it is now or never – and to raise the priority of these demands far above everyday concerns. When the Egyptian police attacked demonstrators, this was interpreted against a background of hope for change, a sense that a historical turning point had arrived. Crowds swelled rather than dissipating.

Crowds can coerce others, intimidating them with numbers and emotions. They can crowd in and stop a vote or, as happened in Florida in 2000, a vote recount. They can block access. They can distract officials and grab important documents, as a Chinese crowd did in 2002, stealing a document they believed proved local government corruption (O'Brien and Li 2006: 86). Sheer numbers have coercive power. After all, if persuasion were the only mechanism, one person could argue the case more cogently than a thousand. Crowds are threats and shows of force even when they do not coerce anyone. Police recognize this, and are intimidated; that is why they so often respond in kind, with their own crowds of officers.

Although in the long run they hope to change others' values, in the short run protestors occasionally want to paralyze or frighten other players through threats. This remains truer for rightwing or religious movements, like the anti-abortion movement in the US, which has tried to alarm abortion doctors into closing their clinics (with remarkable success: 87 percent of US counties have no abortion provider). Most movements of the left adhere to internal democracy and external persuasion as basic values. But there are still cases, like the Egyptian revolution, when protestors fight back. The naughty or nice dilemma persists.

The world's nastiest regimes are often impervious to persuasion, and desperation leads to sabotage and warfare. Nelson Mandela, head of the African National Congress and a global hero for his decades-long struggle against apartheid in South Africa, was the co-founder and head of the ANC's guerrilla force, Umkhonto we Sizwe (Spear of the Nation). This group, founded in 1961, began by blowing up government facilities and infrastructure. But the Afrikaner regime's intransigence eventually led them from sabotage to attacks on civilians in the 1980s: almost weekly assaults on restaurants, amusement parks, crowded city streets, as well as military installations and fuel depots. Black townships became violently ungoverned, generating appalling images on the international news. Only then did global banks begin to withhold their business loans; only then did the regime begin to negotiate with Mandela, releasing him in 1990. Sometimes, only dirty hands can bring success.

Protestors always have several arenas to choose from, and these pose dilemmas. Should they attend to building their internal networks and solidarities, or should they engage opponents, in the Janus dilemma? Should they adopt disruptive, disreputable tactics that involve higher risks, or stick to familiar, legal tactics, in naughty or nice? Facebook groups, friends, and likes do not bring down corrupt regimes; occupying central squares and scaring off the police do. But nice tactics can do other things, like reconfigure a group's reputation.

There is also a **basket dilemma**: should you concentrate all your time and attention in one promising arena, or carry out activities in several arenas? For instance, should you pursue media attention, but also work behind the scenes to negotiate with sympathetic politicians? Should you boycott an election (as Morsi's opponents did in April 2013), but also bring lawsuits to try to stop or delay it? Small protest groups must often concentrate on one tactic, while larger ones have more options.

Boycotting an election raises a more general strategic dilemma that I call "**Being There**": you can try to make an arena seem illegitimate by refusing to participate in it, but you also prevent yourself from having much impact on what goes on inside the arena. This is another dilemma involving risk: a boycott is a gamble that, by not participating, you can destroy the credibility or influence of that arena. If you do not, you must watch the results from the outside, and it is sometimes hard to get back into the arena.

Arena switching is most common when a player has been altogether blocked in one arena, but it also occurs when players calculate that their chances are better in some other setting. You lose a lawsuit and decide that the courts were not a neutral arena but a player with its own, contrary interests; you then appeal to the media and legislatures to change the laws that the courts used to reject your claims. Some arenas are tightly linked in a hierarchy, with an accepted progression from one to another: you lose in one court and appeal to a higher court. Others are loosely linked: once Mubarak had resigned, protestors turned their attention to the elections that would follow.

Structural changes in the rules of arenas are the ultimate goal of big protest movements, which hope to make their own future actions easier. We saw this plainly with the "Wilkes and Liberty" movement, which was trying to craft basic civil liberties, but it is just as clear in Egypt, where protestors wanted radical reforms of the arenas of the state. The 1960s US women's movement pursued laws that would create legal arenas where they could sue for economic justice, having already won the right to vote in 1920.

Some tactics unfold in **secret arenas**, which may or may not result in public revelations. Thus spies – more often employed by the police but sometimes also sent by protest movements – try to work undetected; going public means the end of their utility as spies. But even corporate spies who infiltrate protest groups may occasionally need to go public, taking evidence to the police that is damning enough to provoke interventions. In the US, corporate spies are not subject to the same entrapment restrictions as the police, so they have been known to aid and encourage an individual to plan or plant bombs in order to discredit the movement she claims to be part of (Jasper and Nelkin 1992: 50).

Secret activities by protestors usually aim at some scandalous **revelation**, like the Anonymous hackers who send corporate emails to Wikileaks. The animal rights movement received a big boost from break-ins and whistleblowers who provided video footage of horrendous laboratory experiments on animals that was never meant to be public.

The audience segregation dilemma

Protest groups (and other players) try to convey different messages to different players. They might want to appear benignly moral to the general public yet appear threatening to their corporate targets. They might assure their members that victory is imminent but appeal to new recruits by portraying everything as urgently up for grabs. Many groups discuss radical goals amongst themselves while embracing moderate demands publicly. But in a world permeated by media, not to mention spies, it is difficult to send different messages to different audiences. Coded language helps, and a distinct language helps even more. But there is always a risk that someone will record you, translate your words, and portray you as deceitful.

The best way to restrict a message to a select audience is to have a code that others cannot understand, but this is difficult in modern politics. Controversial orators may use *coded language* that their supporters understand but journalists do not – or at least the most controversial meanings can be denied if necessary. Another case is oppressed groups who literally speak another language, like the indigenous peoples of Latin America. They often broadcast programs in their own languages that Spanish speakers cannot understand. In response, the Ecuadorean government tried to curtail these broadcasts, apprehensive about subversive messages or at least insubordinate tones. Even these broadcasters run the risk that someone will translate their words into Spanish, making them available to audiences for whom they were definitely not intended.

Persuading others

Despite occasional engagements with the coercive forces of order or their own resort to aggressive or even violent tactics, protestors' main activity consists of persuasion: trying to arouse helpful beliefs, feelings, and actions in other players, as well as in their own members.

Protest complicates democracy, at least the democracy of voting for candidates and referenda. It offers other ways of expressing urgent opinions that voting cannot accommodate. The media and politicians are well aware of the costs of different forms of voice, and weigh them accordingly. Signing an online petition may only take a few seconds, emailing a legislator a few minutes; going to a rally may occupy several hours, while getting arrested could take several days. Founding, running, or working for a protest group, or a series of groups, can take a lifetime – undeniable proof of deep moral commitment.

Charles Tilly (2008), recognizing near the end of his life that cultural persuasion is the core of what social movements do, suggested that protestors engage in **WUNC displays** for others: they try to demonstrate their moral Worth, their Unity, their large Numbers, and their great Commitment to the cause. This ungainly but memorable acronym may be Tilly's most lasting concept. WUNC displays are character work: moral worth and commitment demonstrate that protestors are good; unanimity and numbers show they are strong (although, in a world that values democracy, numbers also show that "the people" are behind the cause, reinforcing its moral legitimacy as well). If their moral assertions fail to persuade, they become dangerous villains; if their claims of strength fail, they look like victims or clowns. In one image, Egyptian protestors made Khaled Said a giant hero, holding up a ridiculous (and tiny) Mubarak. Character work, recall, is a key arena, in which players try to portray themselves in a good light and their opponents in a bad light.

The bystanders who watch demonstrators march past – or see them on television – are not the only audience, of course. All the other players are watching as well, if indirectly, even when they are thousands of miles away, like the international human rights groups (a type of international non-governmental organization, or INGO), which bring attention (and often funding) to local groups. Because global capitalism has left us with rich countries and poor countries, the donors are usually in the rich countries

Heroes are large, minions tiny. Credit: Carlos Latuff, Wikimedia Commons.

and those asking for funds are in the poor. A group knows that if it can draw the attention of a prominent organization like Amnesty International, it will also attract media coverage, donations, and diplomatic support. Groups like Amnesty are opinion leaders for other players.

Political scientist Clifford Bob (2005) has studied how INGOs and local insurgents "match up" with one another. The insurgents must craft an identity as "the right kind" of people for the INGO to support, which often means they are the victims of a large multinational corporation (especially one that has created an environmental catastrophe), that they have faced repression from their own government, but also that they have not committed violent acts as part of their own protest. They must be pure victims, with no part of the villain mixed in. The character work that protest groups do in order to appeal to INGOs thus constrains the tactics they can use against their own governments, pushing them down the nice path instead of the naughty. In addition to character work, the supplicants are more likely to get the attention of an INGO if they have a charismatic leader who writes and speaks English well (or whatever language the INGO uses), and if that person either is a celebrity or travels a lot. Personal contacts, the ability to sit down face to face, help a lot.

Just as you try to put on your best moral face, so one of the best ways to undermine your opponents is to raise doubts about their morality. This is just as true for governments as for protestors. The forces of order justify their actions by portraying protestors as disorderly, even criminal in extreme cases. In Egypt this character work failed, so the collapsing regime took an additional step: it withdrew police from the streets and emptied several notorious prisons. Gangs of newly free criminals looted malls and burned cars. "Anarchy," the government newspapers screamed, trying to conflate protestors and criminals. Efforts to appeal to the fears of average folk often succeed, but the Mubarak regime lacked sufficient credibility, or time, to pull it off.

When he was not portraying protestors as immoral and dangerous, Mubarak's other rhetorical strategy was to paint them as weak, ineffectual, and destined to fail, a view that under normal circumstances might deflate protestors' own confidence. This approach works best before your opponents have occupied large squares, set fire to buildings, overturned police cars, and taken other actions that prove their strength. It is the same character work that regimes throughout the world undertake to dismiss protestors as laughable – and one of the ways in which naughty tactics can have a positive effect, establishing the strength of the movement.

Another way to taint your opponents' moral reputation is to catch them in a lie, for nothing stains an organization's or an individual's reputation more. When it tried to portray demonstrators as ineffectual, the Mubarak regime was quickly found out: Al Jazeera television displayed the calm street scene being broadcast on state television next to the actual chaos of gunshots and a burning police van. (In a similar case Syrian activists observed that the "man in the street" who appeared on official state television praising the Assad regime looked familiar; they managed to compile a video with 20 instances when he had been "randomly" chosen to represent public opinion!) When uncovered, lies – and clumsy news manipulation – are among the worst blunders, for you lose not just your credibility but a more general reputation for good intentions. Moral players do not lie.

* * *

Players go at each other, in a complicated sequence of anticipations, moves, countermoves, vetoes, alliances, character work, symbol creation, and more, spilling across multiple arenas where decisions can be made or opinions formed. These strategic games mix calculations and emotions, seductions and threats, persuasion and coercion. They are always complicated. But they determine which players will get what they want, which ones will lose, which will be eliminated altogether, which will endure for the next contest. These engagements are the heart of politics.

Most social movements do not win or lose: they are not crushed and punished, but neither do they attain all the policies and structural changes they had wanted. If movements primarily have to do with persuasion, their major impact, if they have one, is often to change how large numbers of people feel and think. The next chapter looks at this type of impact, in addition to other successes and failures.

8

Winning, Losing, and More

Part of the family: animal rights

Before the nineteenth century, animals were nothing more than a resource: to be eaten, ridden, worn, or destroyed for human amusement, as in cock-fighting or bull-baiting. A handful of dogs were alone lucky enough to be incorporated into the household as a beloved part of the family, mostly by aristocrats who used them for hunting (in Europe) or lap ornaments (in China).

Then, in the industrializing countries of the nineteenth century, the burgeoning middle classes adopted more and more animals (cats as well as dogs) as part of the family, pets to be loved and coddled and not eaten. Societies for the protection of animals began in Britain as an upper-class cause, but for that very reason they had a broad influence. By the 1860s they had spread across Europe and to the US, often through the efforts of British expatriates. These humane societies, which handled strays and investigated cruelty complaints in big cities, were joined later in the century by anti-vivisection societies that produced tracts against experiments on live animals, again starting in Britain.

A century later, in the 1970s in Britain and the 1980s in the US, a more radical animal rights movement emerged, demanding a much broader range of protections for nonhuman species (Jasper and Nelkin 1992). The initial core was a handful of philosophers living or studying in Britain. Part of the impetus came from better scientific knowledge about the cognitive capacities of apes, dolphins, and other species, which made it easier to imagine what their lives feel like to them, and how deprived they must feel when captured, enslaved, and tortured by humans. Another contributing factor was an ecological awareness that the world had not been created for humans to ransack according to their own whims, but consisted of delicate habitats that supported plant and animal species which were disappearing fast.

The new issues went far beyond the abuse of "man's best friend" or the whipping of carriage horses that had exercised nineteenth-century activists, to include hunting, the horrendous conditions in factory farms, the dull routines of animals in circuses and zoos, the use (often required by law) of guinea pigs and other rodents to test new cosmetics and toxic substances. Science had been an issue in the nineteenth century, but its vast expansion in the twentieth had found more and more uses for animals, especially the furry mammals that so easily attract sympathy.

Of all the targets of the animal rights movement, scientists defended themselves most loudly, perhaps because university research labs were frequent targets, and several damning videos of animal suffering were stolen from these labs by spies or burglars in the early 1980s. Animal protectionists ran circles around the scientists' arguments. If animals can feel pain just as we do, how can we justify forcing them to suffer when we would not do the same thing to other humans? At least other humans can consent to pain if they believe there is greater good to come from it. The best that scientists could do was to organize press conferences with winsome children whose lives had been saved by techniques developed and tested on other species, although activists were quick to point out that the same techniques might have – under different laws and scientific norms – been developed without the use of animals, or at least with fewer animals. If scientists struggled to justify their use of animals, the fur coat and other industries barely even tried. They simply donated money to legislators to try to block the most radical proposals.

Britain has passed a series of acts protecting animals in science, beginning in 1986 with mammals, then including octopi (1993), and later fish and amphibians. With these added to its protections for farm animals and general anti-cruelty laws, the UK has the strictest protections in the world. A 2004 law severely restricted fox hunting. The United States in the 1990s also saw a spate of new federal and state laws, as well as amendments to laws first passed around 1900, and extensive regulations governing the treatment of animals on farms and in science, many of them based on scientists' own research into animals' capacities, lives in the wild, and ability to feel pain. Several European nations, soon followed by the European Union, imposed even more stringent laws a few years later. No uses of animals were altogether abolished, but suffering was considerably reduced. Yet people still eat meat, wear fur coats, visit zoos, and buy pets from "puppy mills."

Social movements have a variety of effects, beginning with whether they win or lose. One of the longest-lasting impacts is on how people view and feel about the world, in other words the creation of a new moral sensibility.

Winning and losing

No movements get everything they want from their (usually long) list of demands and hopes. A few attain their major goal, and others realize minor objectives. Most citizenship movements have obtained – after long struggles – the bundle of rights for their members, especially voting, that they were after. It is difficult for systems that call themselves democratic to continue to exclude broad categories of humans from the polity. But even groups that receive the right to vote often face a further series of exclusions and stereotypes that hinder their progress. Women won the right to vote in most democratic nations a century ago, yet had to launch successive waves of protest to be taken seriously in many other arenas. It is one thing to vote, another to become a prime minister.

Post-citizenship movements have a worse track record, because most of them are fighting to change deeply held tastes and attitudes. For full success, the animal rights movement would have to persuade us all to give up not just furs and zoos, but also eating meat. That is a large industry to kill off, no matter how logical or sympathetic the arguments. Many people are aware of the contra-dictions in their lifestyles, but contradictions are not sufficient to change engrained habits.

It is more usual for a movement to swing policies slightly in a favorable direction than to win its explicit goals. Laws and policies emerge from a complex web of political arenas, in which protest movements are usually fairly weak players compared to political parties, corporations, and public opinion as purveyed through the media. Parties and movements interact with each other in complex ways: individuals move back and forth, movements penetrate or create parties, parties and movements form alliances, parties co-opt movement issues with or without giving credit to the move-ments. In any case, politicians and bureaucrats must see some advantage in accommodating movement demands, whether this involves more votes, new coalitions, or greater funding for their agencies; or they need to fear that the movement can disrupt their goals, such as maintaining order. Like other players, politicians can be persuaded, bought off, or coerced.

Because their audiences are fragmented, protestors don't always know what rhetorical effect they are having on any one of them. This is especially true when they target politicians, who occasion-ally embrace a cause but who also have a stake in denying that non-institutional tactics influence policies. Nonetheless, legisla-tion and court decisions, no matter how much they are presented as being unaffected by outsiders, sometimes shift in directions favored by protestors. Old people's movements in the 1930s encouraged the US Congress to pass the Social Security Act; anti-war demonstrators in the 1960s had more effect on the White House than they realized at the time. Politicians have a knack for co-opting issues and the feelings behind them while denying they are doing so (Amenta 2006).

Protest groups can influence policies at different stages: when agendas are set, when the content of a new law is written, when it is voted upon and signed, or when it is implemented (Amenta and Young 1999). The most successful movements change the rules of arenas in ways that make it easier for them to influence future

The articulation dilemma

It might seem as though movements need to be clear about their goals, if they are ever going to attain them. They often focus on laws or policies they would like to see enacted or abolished. A clear goal attracts those who agree with it. But there is also a downside to clear articulation: those who do not share that precise goal may avoid the movement, even if they favor related goals. And once the narrow goal is attained, what does a movement do next? Are there associated goals to which it should redirect attention? Can it manage to avoid the demobilization that often follows the attainment of a stated goal? Plus, a clear goal can stimulate vigorous action by the intended targets, or by political parties that can attract voters who disagree with that goal.

decisions, granting them some kind of standing. This often takes the form of a new state agency that comes to "own" the social problem that the movement has publicized: environmental protection, consumer fraud, women's bureaus, pensions, workplace safety, child protection, and so forth. In many cases, state officials themselves desire reforms, and can use evidence of popular support to pursue their own goals, encouraging or even funding protest organizations.

Protest is usually one part of social change, reflecting but also furthering new sensibilities, encouraged by state players but also aiding them. Some movements are asking for things that would happen anyway, but they may speed the process along, helping people figure out what they want. On the other hand, when they enter political arenas, where competition between parties is the rule, explicit demands may instead arouse opposition, slowing the process of change. Your opponents will try to block your proposals, if only to damage you. This is why so many movements have their main impacts outside political arenas.

Like individuals, social movements have many goals they would like to accomplish. Some are stated and others not; some are the hopes of factions and individuals, while others are widely supported; different goals come to the forefront when they seem easier to obtain and recede when they seem difficult. Strategic interactions are unpredictable, and it often turns out that a group's original goals are no longer possible or desirable. It may turn to more modest objectives, or, conversely, it may take advantage of openings to push for more ambitious ones.

The Egyptian revolution succeeded because such diverse people were attracted to it, united only in their hatred of Mubarak and disagreeing entirely over what should replace him (one no, many yeses). The Tahrir protestors were united by their emotions more than by their ideologies, but that was enough to topple one of the world's strongest dictators. The Occupy movement, too, shared a mood of indignation over economic inequality, but refused to state policy goals. Mission statements, promulgated to the world, are not easily undone, tying the hands of later decision-making assemblies. This is one of the reasons that Occupy Wall Street was reluctant to formulate its demands, since members realized that they had shown up for many different reasons, but also that future General Assemblies might have different goals. They felt they could not decide for GAs to come. "We're here, we're unclear, get used to it."

Inspiring others

Social movements affect each other. Protestors in one movement are often involved in other ones as well; they know people in them, and they borrow ideas, symbols, and tactics. All sorts of information and emotion flow along networks of activists that cut across movements. Protest groups can also form alliances, explicitly sharing their visions and, in rare cases, resources. But the main way that one group affects others, or one movement influences others, is through emotional inspiration. "Look at them. They are doing something wonderful. We should too." This requires some admiration and identification with those others.

The negative counterpart is when another movement does

something outrageous or threatening, and you must act in response. The US Christian Right, as we saw, emerged from older groups and churches in response to both feminism and LGBTQ activism.

Because state players are so important, one protest group observes other groups for signs about how the police, courts, and other agencies are likely to react to protest. Nasty repression can have a broadly chilling effect. But when a government accepts the demands of one group, this can encourage others to make similar demands, just as women's rights have often surfaced in the US during movements for black civil rights. This information is hardly perfect, as the forces of order may tolerate or even encourage one movement while coming down hard on another.

Because old movements inspire new ones, protest movements often cluster in **protest waves**. Students, workers, ecologists, feminists, racial-ethnic groups, and others took to the streets in the late 1960s and early 1970s across a variety of nations, especially but not only in Europe. Each group inspired the others, and individuals moved among movements. Another wave began in the late 1990s, becoming known as the global justice movement. The Occupy and Indignados movements of 2011 were an additional, very sudden, cluster, but they also can be seen as part of the longer global justice wave.

Structural theories see not only waves, but cycles, in which each stage of the cycle leads to the next stage, over and over. The mechanism is that the political system has generally weakened, and movements arise to take advantage of the opportunities, observing each other only for clues as to where the openings are; eventually the state regroups and suppresses protest; later the cycle starts again as memories of repression fade. A more rationalist account of waves sees protestors as carefully calculating their odds of success and the odds of repression, based on what happens to other movements when they go into the streets. In a more cultural take on protest waves, one protest movement inspires others through an appealing moral vision, emotions such as hope and excitement, and usually a shared frame and beliefs.

We must be cautious in talking about waves of protest, because we risk adopting the perspective of the media or even the police without realizing it, since they are our usual source of information about how much protest there is at any given moment. We do not want to overlook all the activity that occurs during quieter times, or times when the media lose interest.

How we think

Movements try to change how we think about the world, helping us to see it in new ways, and to see new things in that world. Participants work out new visions first for themselves but then offer them to the rest of us. Sometimes the main purpose of a movement is to give a name to a social problem: persuading people that sexism, sexual harassment, animal cruelty, racism, institutional racism, child sexual abuse, global injustice, and other problems exist. With a label, they can be recognized, measured, and perhaps monitored. After their reality is established, protestors and their allies can demonstrate the harm they do, and the urgency of stopping them. Expertise can be created for dealing with them. Through their character work, social movements can leave behind new patterns of blame, new villains and victims.

Social movements often help us think of *ourselves* in new ways, especially as part of a new collective identity. Many movements try to revise identities that already exist – African Americans, women, gays and lesbians, the working class – while others try to create new identities by identifying social problems, such as "battered women" or survivors of sexual abuse. Ecology, animal rights, and a few other movements try to expand our circle of moral concern outward to encompass nonhuman nature. Their collective identities are less clearly bounded, but the point is that humans should "decenter" themselves, seeing themselves as a small part of a big universe. If this is the goal, the tactics for getting there may nonetheless rely on movement identities: we are proud of fighting for animals, of being compassionate yet politically tough. We develop new identities as "ecologists" or "animal rights activists."

Some movements even alter basic *science* and *technology*. One of ACT UP's central concerns was to speed up drug trials, and in fact it transformed the way that urgently needed drugs are tested in the US. There would be little recycling or wind power in the world today without the prod of the environmental movement. Animal rights activists shook up the complacent routines of scientists, especially those using live animal trials like the Draize test, in which potential irritants are put in the eyes of conscious, restrained animals – mostly white rabbits – to look for signs of inflammation. Photos of these animals, with their eyes bleeding, inflamed a bright red, or oozing yellow pus, were powerful recruiting tools for the movement. In the controversy that arose, it turned out that these tests, around for decades, continued primarily because national laws required them for many kinds of new substances. Some questioned whether rabbit and human eyes were similar enough.

Within a decade, alternative tests were developed using skin cells, and the Draize test itself was modified to use diluted forms of a substance, to stop at the first sign of irritation, and to begin with just one animal rather than a whole battery of them. The Home Office in the UK imposed a number of tight restrictions in 2006, including that other tests must be tried first; the secretary of state must approve any exceptions. Suffering was vastly reduced, and the science of testing advanced.

How we feel

Movements also affect our feelings, such as what arouses indignation or compassion, what makes us proud or ashamed. Certain aspects of emotions can be changed, others cannot. Humans have biological capacities to produce adrenaline, to raise our heartbeats, to blush, flex our muscles, and more – the basic feeling-thinking processes that make up emotions. These are not in themselves cultural products. But we saw earlier that a lot *is* culturally determined: what *triggers* these actions, what *labels* we apply to these bundles of feelings, and how we *display* what we are feeling.

Protest movements have helped change our very bodily urges, or at least their expressions. For some individuals, children may remain objects of lust, but protection movements have increased the penalties for acting upon that lust. Other movements have increased the costs of certain substance addictions. The anti-smoking movement has been enormously successful in the last two decades, limiting the spread of the urge itself rather than its expression. Anti-smoking commercials link tobacco to frightening health outcomes, in an effort to make us disgusted by tobacco. Vegetarians try hard to promote disgust with meat products.

Social movements have also fought to control bodily urges associated with pain. In politics, our urges are sometimes used against us, as in techniques of torture that take advantage not only of pain but of related urges such as the need to sleep or defecate. The elimination of pain from police repertories has been a goal of movement after movement for hundreds of years, and the contemporary human rights movement is one of the world's largest protest efforts – a sign that, despite much progress, there is still a lot to be done in the fight against torture.

Social movements have also affected our reflex emotions. Disgust has been constrained, for instance. We are still disgusted by rotten eggs or slimy secretions, but less often by entire categories of people. In most countries, women are no longer considered disgusting when they menstruate, Jews are no longer thought to be dirty and smelly, as anti-Semites once perceived them. Most people, most of the time, have a broader view of who is fully human than their ancestors did, a triumph for civilization.

Even anger, which would seem to be an emotion that is urgent and automatic, is displayed in different ways in different cultures. It has been curtailed in many situations: a man who hits his wife can be arrested now. Over time, such men learn to control themselves. In the 250 years since Wilkes's supporters marched through England's cities, protestors have also learned to curtail public displays of anger; in most demonstrations they appear calm and controlled, even though they are indignant about some government decision or social problem.

On the other hand, some groups discover the power and even joy of anger through protest, moving in the opposite direction

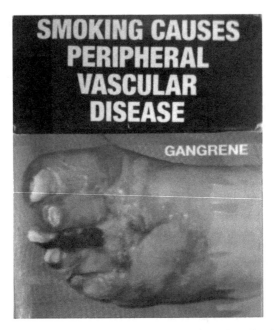

New Australian cigarette package aimed at teaching us to be disgusted.
Credit: Marco Nembrini.

along the naughty or nice dilemma. The women's movement had to battle the traditional expectations that women were not supposed to be angry, a limitation that made it hard to mobilize a movement on their own behalf. Subordinate groups have to be able to feel and display some aggressive emotions if they are to get their way. Emotional expressions of various sorts are fundamental to politics.

Social movements have a big impact on our enduring affective commitments. We noted how they create new identities for us, new patterns of love and hate. Nationalism is not always pretty, but nationalist movements have been among the most successful in history. In many cases, such as LGBTQ and the Dalits, the first goal of a movement is to transform group shame into pride, a basic sense of human dignity. The life of groups is central to our humanity, and an emotional as well as cognitive creation.

Art is a moving combination of thinking and feeling, and a number of movements have left behind great art, including music, paintings, novels, and poetry. Protestors and artists share an exhilarating feeling that they are creating a new world, developing new imagery and language to express a vision that has not yet crystalized. Together they articulate the new sensibility. Protest is itself artful (Jasper 1997).

The moral impact

Ultimately, movements help members – and others – to articulate and extend new moral visions, based on new ways of feeling and thinking. The basic **dignity** of all people, with a variety of rights – civil, political, economic – has been promoted by protest movements around the world, with participants usually demanding such rights for themselves but also sometimes demanding them for others (although a central component of dignity is to demand your own rights if you can). These rights are always ends in themselves, but they are also the means for pursuing additional goals, even additional rights. Once women and the working class had attained the right to vote, they could pursue economic protections and advancement more easily. The core of human dignity is to be able to control the world around you rather than to be controlled by others or buffeted by fate.

Dignity is so important to people that they will protest as a way of obtaining it even against frightening odds (Wood 2003). They may not think they have any chance of winning, but the mere fact of getting into the street to assert their moral voice outweighs the risks. Their bravery, standing in front of tanks and armed troops, police dogs and water cannons, is breathtaking. There are moral "hypergoods," valued at a deeper level than other desirable things, that are sometimes worth more than life itself (Taylor 1989).

Social movements affect both moral principles and intuitions, on the one hand, and the emotions that result from them, on the other. We are capable of more indignation as we include more

179

groups of people – or other species – within our circle of moral concern, as we come to care about them as morally valuable. As we have more mechanisms for redressing grievances at our disposal, we have more opportunities to articulate and act upon our outrage. The realm of God and Nature shrinks, the realm of human choice – where blame, indignation, and revenge are possible – expands.

Compassion – the empathic ability to feel something of what another being is feeling – may be the clearest moral legacy that generations of activists have left us. Animal protection was a big step forward in the nineteenth century, predating women's suffrage and freedom for African slaves, and even lending its model to the child protection movement. In the long perspective of history, the extension of compassion and the elaboration of our sense of fairness might have happened anyway, even without social movements to promote them. Some historians believe that capitalism changed our moral visions by making us aware of distant suffering and the economic systems that connect us all (Haskell 1985). But activists have certainly helped, as someone had to articulate those new intuitions, promote the new laws, and challenge obsolete practices.

How we act

New ways of thinking, feeling, and judging often lead to new practices, from more humane farming to participation for once-marginal groups. Conscious strategic action leads to the creation of new habits and bureaucratic routines that then no longer need to be explicitly evaluated and debated. They fade into the taken-for-granted background of life. Women vote. Decent people do not beat their dogs, or their children, or their partners.

Although most protestors would love to change how everyone in their society or the entire world thinks, feels, and acts, the biggest impact of their activity is usually on their own lives. The **biographical consequences** of participation are lifelong. Researchers have looked at those who were active during the 1960s, finding that they continue to follow politics more closely, care more about what they consume, and participate in today's movements more than members of the same generation who were not active. Activists develop confidence, critical thinking, and political know-how that they never lose, even during quiet periods of their lives. They are quick to join a new cause when a sympathetic one arises. Their lives have been changed forever (McAdam 1988).

This impact on participants is part of a broader way in which movements affect action: they develop new methods of doing politics. The tactics of protest change with each movement, and sometimes even faster than that, as protestors learn new ways to carry out their own activities. Gandhi mixed Jainist and other ideas to forge a nonviolent movement that, partly because of its success, inspired many other movements in the second half of the twentieth century (Nepstad 2011). Nonviolent activists developed participatory democracy in the 1960s, followed by consensus decision-making in the 1970s and 1980s. Techniques for acting and deciding while remaining true to basic moral principles have proliferated in the years since, allowing social forums and general assemblies to flourish. How could movements yearning for social change not try to change themselves first?

These new ways of making decisions are linked to compassion. By putting aside simple voting, consensus and related techniques are efforts to force people to listen to each other, across differences of background, experience, social location, and even political preferences. Others must be taken seriously as players to persuade, not coerce, but also as sources of new ideas and stories. They are not canon fodder to be manipulated and used up as resources. They are dignified ends in themselves.

Writing history

The final arena in most social conflicts is the battle over how to write the history of the conflict. Protestors seek evidence of influence and progress, giving hope to future mobilizations and validating their powerful feeling of "making history." Since they rarely get all that they want, they may also need to craft a story about why they lost, sometimes blaming villainous opponents who were too well entrenched, too rich and powerful, or too devious to overcome – this time. Articles appear debating these issues even while a movement is declining; books – many of them former PhD dissertations – arrive a few years later. Prominent conflicts are food for thought decades later.

Every movement's fate is a lesson for future movements, contributing to a narrative of history, to our common sense about politics and change. In retrospect, certain events turn out to have been pivotal moments, for good or bad, which need to be understood. We try to place them in the context of broader struggles and history in order to move forward.

For movements that were not notably successful, former participants sometimes find a glimmer of hope by redefining what the original goals were: instead of full recognition or policies reflecting all the movement's goals, it turns out the movement was aiming at public awareness all along. Everyone can be a hero. Conveniently, shifting cultural understandings are indeed the biggest legacy of most social movements.

When activists write history, they typically portray themselves as heroes, their opponents as villains. To be heroic is to have an impact, and they frequently exaggerate their own effects. Mainstream politicians, on the other hand, tend to downplay the influence of movements, naturally giving themselves more of the credit for solving society's problems. Corporations and other frequent targets of protest tend to portray the efforts of *both* protestors *and* politicians as misguided, doing more harm than good. The mainstream news media usually take the politicians' view, embracing political reform from within the system while portraying radical protestors as entertaining kooks.

Ironically, former protestors and mainstream observers sometimes converge on the same distortions of the past (Ross 2002). Past conflicts tend to be framed as part of the long advance of human rights, since this allows protestors to assert their influence and politicians to praise the system's capacity for reform. Violent tactics are often ignored, as most protestors prefer to embrace nonviolence; mainstream observers hesitate to remind young generations of activists that violence is a possibility, and often a successful tactic. Former rebels – now respected politicians, parents, or members of their communities – may have an interest in concealing their own radical pasts.

* * *

Social movements are never the only force at work in social change. They interact with public opinion, shifting sensibilities, works of art, policy arenas. Often, they are both the offspring of shifting visions and their midwives. They may single out sources of resistance to change, such as obsolete practices like the Draize test. Persuasion happens in little steps: a person is moved by a frame, attracted to an activist, enveloped by a moral vision with its patterns of hope and indignation.

Social change also arrives in little steps, most of the time. When it happens suddenly, it usually comes by means of force rather than persuasion. Sometimes violence has the desired effect, in the short run. More often it spins out of control. Those with power, like the Egyptian army, do not like to give it up. New laws seem to bring fast changes, but they are often the end result of deeper cultural transformations. As symbolic statements, they contribute to the underlying sensibility as well as reflecting it.

Many of the routines we follow in daily life reflect political conflicts of the past: how many hours we work in a day, the foods we eat and what is in them, who goes to school and what they learn there, the medicines and technologies available when we are sick, the respect we give to doctors but not to nurses, the transportation systems that move us around, our spiritual sensibilities, our sources of electricity and heat, and more. Protestors lose as many battles as they win, and often combine some wins and some losses, but their efforts have created our worlds. This kind of impact is the definition of a hero.

Conclusion: Humans as Heroes

In late 2011, I went to Florence for a dissertation defense and a panel on protest, but also spent a couple days visiting tourist sights. I sought out the serene arcaded square designed by the amazing Filippo Brunelleschi in 1419, a key moment in the invention of public spaces during the Renaissance. To my delight, Occupy Florence had its encampment in one corner of the square, facing off against a handicraft jewelry market in the opposite corner. A professional flutist was serenading three or four Occupiers, including a young boy blowing his whistle randomly and annoyingly. Protest is everywhere, from the brutal concrete of Zuccotti Park to the lovely squares of Tuscany, birthplace of the modern public space. It is woven deeply into the fabric of modern democracy, basic human rights, and contemporary culture. It protects, extends, and creates all of these.

Culture helps us to act in the world as well as to understand it. We relate to our social, psychological, physical (and spiritual) contexts partly through feeling our way around them, using our emotions as our guides. Social movements help us work out new ways of doing, of treating each other, of imagining new futures, new inspirations and hopes, new symbols, characters, and other guideposts we can use along the way to the future. They even help us develop new ways of being in our own bodies, of being human even at this basic level.

Human action is full of dilemmas and tradeoffs, and so we are constantly juggling many goals, many means, and many different viewpoints. Only rarely and temporarily are large groups able to speak with one voice, as they do in social movements. It is a great human accomplishment, but always fragile and fleeting. And that unity is not always a good thing, since not all movements are good: the Nazis and other fascist movements were extremely unified.

Protestors are real human beings, with decisions to make, habits they form, desires that are sometimes admirable and sometimes not. They are capable of heroic actions, but also disappointing or mistaken actions. Most theories of protest have offered stick figures, going through predictable emotions, melting into the crowd, driven by a single motivation. We would not want to be portrayed like that, and protestors do not either. Theories are always simplifications, but cultural theories are less crude than most, because their starting point is the subjects' point of view, their feelings and goals and actions, the choices they make as they try to get their way. Other theories start by reducing them to stick figures; cultural theories at least try to avoid doing that.

My first loyalty as a writer is to my readers, but I also owe something to the protestors I write about. I do not owe them admiration and loyalty, because I do not admire or agree with all of them. With some movements, in fact, I sharply disagree. But I owe all the participants some compassion, as complex human beings, which amounts to a respect for their dignity. Even Hitler was human, and we can only understand his troubled mind through its human motivations and failings. In other books, I have often written about individual activists, in the hopes of respecting their full complexity, even though words on a page can never express a person's human fullness. Even more than respect, I think I owe them the truth. We need to be as accurate as we can when we describe protest, getting the details down as well as possible. We have to try constantly to get it right, fighting our own biases and laziness.

This is the danger of Big History theories: they already know what protestors want, or should want, what the function of this or that movement must be. The theory gets in the way of watching and listening as the protestors themselves figure out what they want. A cultural approach, in contrast, is the intellectual's equivalent of consensus process, in which everyone is required to listen to others. It is a compassionate ideal that we may never completely attain; but we must never give up trying.

We express our discontent in many ways, and social movements are actually rare compared to many other ways. They are hard to assemble and maintain, requiring lots of time and attention. But when they happen, they feel like the highest purpose of humanity, at least in this world, a triumph of cooperation, moral vision, and fellowship. Social movements are a great laboratory for understanding how people come together to cooperate, voluntarily, for some common purpose. This is rare enough, but rarer still when people do this without getting paid for it. This collective action is the essence of social life: how can people trust one another, put aside coercion in favor of persuasion, and place collective projects above their own individual and family concerns? Those visions and projects are the most deeply moving of all human motivations.

Although it is reassuring to think that social movements represent gradual progress toward social justice and equality, people can band together for any sort of goal, vicious as well as sympathetic. But when progress is made, it is always because social movements have formed and prodded the rest of their society, the rest of the world, to follow along. They are necessary although not sufficient for progress. Social justice depends on social movements. Those in privileged positions rarely give up their advantages without a fight.

We began this book by wondering what protestors are like, why they undertake the costly, risky projects that they often do. The brief answer is, they are just like you and me. Any one of us could end up in the street, because we all have something we care about so much that threats to it could shock us into indignation. And with the right combination of personal contacts, organizations and resources, inspiring symbols and leaders, and everything else we have looked at in this book, we could find ourselves in the middle of a social movement, even leading one. Protestors *are* you and me.

References and Suggested Readings
(marked with *)

*Alexander, Jeffrey C. 2011. *Performative Revolution in Egypt*. London: Bloomsbury Academic. *A famous social theorist traces the battle over images and meanings through the lens of politics as public performance.*

Amenta, Edwin. 2006. *When Movements Matter*. Princeton: Princeton University Press.

Amenta, Edwin, and Michael P. Young. 1999. "Making an Impact." In Marco Giugni, Doug McAdam, and Charles Tilly, eds., *How Movements Matter*. Minneapolis: University of Minnesota Press.

Bagdikian, Ben H. 2004. *The New Media Monopoly*. Boston: Beacon Press.

Benford, Robert D. 1997. "An Insider's Critique of the Social Movement Framing Perspective." *Sociological Inquiry* 67: 409–430.

Bernstein, Mary C. 1997. "Celebration and Suppression." *American Journal of Sociology* 103: 531–565.

Blee, Kathleen M. 2012. *Democracy in the Making: How Activists Form Groups*. New York: Oxford University Press.

*Bob, Clifford. 2005. *The Marketing of Rebellion*. Cambridge: Cambridge University Press. *Insurgents sell themselves to international donors through charismatic leaders and constructing the right character as victims.*

Bob, Clifford. 2012. *The Global Right Wing and the Clash of World Politics*. Cambridge: Cambridge University Press.

Breines, Wini. 1982. *Community and Organization in the New Left, 1962–1968*. New York: Praeger.

*Castells, Manuel. 2009. *Communication Power*. Oxford: Oxford University Press. *New communication networks and media have reshaped politics and protest.*

Castells, Manuel. 2012. *Networks of Outrage and Hope*. Cambridge: Polity.

Chauncey, George. 1994. *Gay New York*. New York: Basic Books.

Collins, Randall. 2001. "Social Movements and the Focus of Emotional Attention." In Jeff Goodwin et al., *Passionate Politics*. Chicago: University of Chicago Press.

References and Suggested Readings

Collins, Randall. 2004. *Interaction Ritual Chains*. Princeton: Princeton University Press.

Coontz, Stephanie. 2011. *A Strange Stirring*. New York: Basic Books.

Dabashi, Hamid. 2012. *The Arab Spring*. London: Zed Books.

Davis, Kathy. 2007. *The Making of Our Bodies, Ourselves*. Durham: Duke University Press.

De Beauvoir, Simone. 2010 [1949]. *The Second Sex*. New York: Knopf.

della Porta, Donatella, Andretta Massimiliano, Lorenzo Mosca, and Herbert Reiter. 2006. *Globalization from Below: Transnational Activists and Protest Networks*. Minneapolis: University of Minnesota Press.

della Porta, Donatella, and Herbert Reiter, eds. 1998. *Policing Protest*. Minneapolis: University of Minnesota Press.

Doerr, Nicole. 2012. "Translating Democracy: How Activists in the European Social Forum Practice Multilingual Deliberation." *European Political Science Review* 4: 361–384.

Doherty, Brian, and Graeme Hayes. 2014. "The Courts: Criminal Trials as Strategic Arenas." In Jan Willem Duyvendak and James M. Jasper, eds., *Breaking Down the State*. Amsterdam: Amsterdam University Press.

*Duyvendak, Jan Willem, and James M. Jasper, eds. 2014. *Players and Arenas* and (2015) *Breaking Down the State*. Amsterdam: Amsterdam University Press. *These two volumes look at most of the other players with whom protestors interact.*

Earl, Jennifer, and Katrina Kimport. 2011. *Digitally Enabled Social Change*. Cambridge: MIT Press.

Evans, Sara. 1979. *Personal Politics*. New York: Knopf.

Evans, Sara, and Harry Boyte. 1986. *Free Spaces*. New York: Harper and Row.

*Eyerman, Ron, and Andrew Jamison. 1991. *Social Movements: A Cognitive Approach*. University Park: Pennsylvania State University Press. *Shows how movements generate new knowledge, even technical and scientific knowledge.*

Eyerman, Ron, and Andrew Jamison. 1998. *Music and Social Movements*. Cambridge: Cambridge University Press.

Fetner, Tina. 2008. *How the Religious Right Shaped Lesbian and Gay Activism*. Minneapolis: University of Minnesota Press.

Fillieule, Olivier. 2010. "Some Elements of an Interactionist Approach to Political Disengagement." *Social Movement Studies* 9: 1–15.

Fillieule, Olivier, and Danielle Tartakowsky. 2013. *Demonstrations*. Winnipeg: Fernwood.

Fine, Gary Alan. 2001. *Difficult Reputations: Collective Memories of the Evil, Inept, and Controversial*. Chicago: University of Chicago Press.

Fine, Gary Alan. 2012. *Tiny Publics*. New York: Russell Sage Foundation.

Fiske, Susan T. 2012. *Envy Up, Scorn Down*. New York: Russell Sage Foundation.

References and Suggested Readings

Freeman, Jo. 1972. "On the Tyranny of Structurelessness." *The Second Wave* 2: 20.

Friedan, Betty. 1963. *The Feminine Mystique*. New York: W. W. Norton & Co.

Gamson, Joshua. 1995. "Must Identity Movements Self-Destruct? A Queer Dilemma." *Social Problems* 42: 390–407.

*Gamson, William A. 1992. *Talking Politics*. Cambridge: Cambridge University Press. *Uses focus groups to show how we construct political meanings from a variety of sources.*

Gamson, William A., and Gadi Wolfsfeld. 1993. "Movements and Media as Interacting Systems." *Annals* 528: 114–125.

Ganz, Marshall. 2000. "Resources and Resourcefulness." *American Journal of Sociology* 105: 1003–1065.

*Gitlin, Todd. 1980. *The Whole World Is Watching*. Berkeley: University of California Press. *A leader of SDS examines the complex interaction between protestors and media, especially demonstrating the media dilemma.*

Gitlin, Todd. 2012. *Occupy Nation*. New York: It Books.

Goldfarb, Jeffrey C. 2006. *The Politics of Small Things*. Chicago: University of Chicago Press.

Goodwin, Jeff. 1997. "The Libidinal Constitution of a High-Risk Social Movement." *American Sociological Review* 62: 53–69.

Goodwin, Jeff. 2001. *No Other Way Out*. Cambridge: Cambridge University Press.

*Goodwin, Jeff, and James M. Jasper, eds. 2014. *The Social Movement Reader*, 3rd edn. Oxford: Wiley. *A collection of basic readings and concept definitions.*

*Goodwin, Jeff, James M. Jasper, and Francesca Polletta, eds. 2001. *Passionate Politics*. Chicago: University of Chicago Press. *Essays on the role of emotions in social movements.*

*Gould, Deborah. 2009. *Moving Politics*. Chicago: University of Chicago Press. *In the exciting story of ACT UP, Gould unearths the many emotions in the rise and also the fall of the protest group.*

Haines, Herbert H. 1988. *Black Radicals and the Civil Rights Mainstream, 1954–1970*. Knoxville: University of Tennessee Press.

Haskell, Thomas. 1985. "Capitalism and the Origins of the Humanitarian Sensibility," parts 1 & 2. *American Historical Review* 90: 339–361, 547–566.

Hebdige, Dick. 1979. *Subculture*. New York: Methuen.

*Jasper, James M. 1997. *The Art of Moral Protest*. Chicago: University of Chicago Press. *Shows many ways that culture permeates protest, including morality, emotions, and cognition.*

*Jasper, James M. 2006. *Getting Your Way: Strategic Dilemmas in the Real World*. Chicago: University of Chicago Press. *More detailed discussion of strategic dilemmas, applied to all sorts of players in addition to protestors.*

References and Suggested Readings

Jasper, James M., and Dorothy Nelkin. 1992. *The Animal Rights Crusade*. New York: Free Press.

*Johnston, Hank, and Bert Klandermans, eds. 1995. *Social Movements and Culture*. Minneapolis: University of Minnesota Press. *An interesting early volume that encouraged the cultural approach to protest.*

Katz, Jonathan Ned. 1995. *The Invention of Heterosexuality*. Chicago: University of Chicago Press.

Kelner, Shaul. 2010. *Tours that Bind*. New York: New York University Press.

Khalil, Karima, ed. 2011. *Messages from Tahrir*. Cairo: American University of Cairo Press.

Klandermans, Bert. 1997. *The Social Psychology of Protest*. Oxford: Blackwell.

Klapp, Orrin E. 1969. *Collective Search for Identity*. New York: Holt, Rinehart, and Winston.

Klimova, Sveta. 2009. "Speech Act Theory and Protest Discourse." In Hank Johnston, ed., *Culture, Social Movements, and Protest*. Burlington: Ashgate.

Kriesi, Hanspeter, Ruud Koopmans, Jan Willem Duyvendak, and Marco Giugni. 1995. *New Social Movements in Western Europe*. Minneapolis: University of Minnesota Press.

Krinsky, John, and Colin Barker. 2009. "Movement Strategizing as Developmental Learning." In Hank Johnston, ed., *Culture, Social Movements, and Protest*. Burlington: Ashgate.

*Lalich, Janja. 2004. *Bounded Choice: True Believers and Charismatic Cults*. Berkeley: University of California Press. *A detailed study of how the leaders of two groups built deep – even suicidal – loyalty among members.*

Leondar-Wright, Betsy. 2014. *Missing Class: How Seeing Class Cultures Can Strengthen Social Movement Groups*. Ithaca: Cornell University Press.

*Lichbach, Mark. 1995. *The Rebel's Dilemma*. Ann Arbor: University of Michigan Press. *By extending the rational-choice approach, Lichbach provides a catalogue of movement dilemmas.*

*Luker, Kristin. 1984. *Abortion and the Politics of Motherhood*. Berkeley: University of California Press. *Although her portrayal of the anti-abortion movement is out of date, her contrast between the two worldviews pitted against one another is a model of interpretative sociology.*

Maeckelbergh, Marianne. 2009. *The Will of the Many*. London: Pluto Press.

*Mansbridge, Jane J. 1986. *Why We Lost the ERA*. Chicago: University of Chicago Press. *An insider's view of some of the dilemmas this giant movement faced, especially how it came to grief over the Janus dilemma.*

Marcus, George E. 2002. *The Sentimental Citizen: Emotion in Democratic Politics*. University Park: Pennsylvania State University Press.

Marsden, George M. 2006. *Fundamentalism and American Culture*, 2nd edn. New York: Oxford University Press.

References and Suggested Readings

McAdam, Doug. 1982. *Political Process and the Development of Black Insurgency, 1890–1970.* Chicago: University of Chicago Press.

McAdam, Doug. 1988. *Freedom Summer.* New York: Oxford University Press.

*McAdam, Doug, Sidney Tarrow, and Charles Tilly. 2001. *Dynamics of Contention.* Cambridge: Cambridge University Press. *Structuralists' own critique of structuralism.*

*McCarthy, John D., and Mayer N. Zald. 1977. "Resource Mobilization and Social Movements: A Partial Theory." *American Journal of Sociology* 82: 1212–1241. *Even though they ignore cultural processes, this is an important article that defined resource mobilization.*

McGarry, Aidan, and James M. Jasper, eds. 2015. *The Identity Dilemma.*

McGirr, Lisa. 2001. *Suburban Warriors.* Princeton: Princeton University Press.

*Melucci, Alberto. 1996. *Challenging Codes.* Cambridge: Cambridge University Press. *Pays special attention to the role of collective identities in almost all aspects of movement life.*

Meyer, David S., and Deana A. Rohlinger. 2012. "Big Books and Social Movements." *Social Problems* 59: 136–153.

Meyer, David S., and Sidney Tarrow, eds. 1997. *The Social Movement Society.* Lanham: Rowman and Littlefield.

Mische, Ann. 2003. "Cross-Talk in Movements." In Mario Diani and Doug McAdam, eds., *Social Movements and Networks.* Oxford: Oxford University Press.

*Morris, Aldon. 1984. *The Origins of the Civil Rights Movement.* New York: Free Press. *Although covering many aspects of the early movement, he is especially good on the cultural materials – songs, Bible references, prayers – that black churches provided.*

Munson, Ziad. 2009. *The Making of Pro-Life Activists.* Chicago: University of Chicago Press.

Nepstad, Sharon Erickson. 2011. *Nonviolent Revolutions.* New York: Oxford University Press.

O'Brien, Kevin J., and Lianjiang Li. 2006. *Rightful Resistance in Rural China.* Cambridge: Cambridge University Press.

Olson, Mancur. 1965. *The Logic of Collective Action.* Cambridge: Harvard University Press.

*Opp, Karl-Dieter. 2009. *Theories of Political Protest and Social Movements.* New York: Routledge. *An effort to incorporate cultural concepts such as collective identity into rational-choice theory.*

Owens, Lynn. 2009. *Cracking under Pressure.* Amsterdam: Amsterdam University Press.

Pinard, Maurice. 2011. *Motivational Dimensions in Social Movements and Contentious Collective Action.* Montreal: McGill-Queen's University Press.

*Piven, Frances Fox, and Richard A. Cloward. 1977. *Poor People's Movements.* New York: Random House. *Disruption is the key.*

Pleyers, Geoffrey. 2010. *Alter-Globalization*. Cambridge: Polity.

*Polletta, Francesca. 2002. *Freedom Is an Endless Meeting*. Chicago: University of Chicago Press. *How protestors negotiate several strategic dilemmas in making decisions.*

*Polletta, Francesca. 2006. *It Was Like a Fever*. Chicago: University of Chicago Press. *The role of narrative in protest.*

Reed, T. V. 2005. *The Art of Protest*. Minneapolis: University of Minnesota Press.

Rosen, Ruth. 2000. *The World Split Open*. New York: Viking.

*Rosenthal, Rob, and Richard Flacks. 2012. *Playing for Change*. Boulder: Paradigm Publishers. *The most thorough book yet on music and movements.*

Ross, Kristin. 2002. *May '68 and its Afterlives*. Chicago: University of Chicago Press.

Rupp, Leila J., and Verta Taylor. 1987. *Survival in the Doldrums*. New York: Oxford University Press.

Sarat, Austin, and Stuart A. Scheingold, eds. 1998. *Cause Lawyering*. Oxford: Oxford University Press.

Scott, James C. 1985. *Weapons of the Weak*. New Haven: Yale University Press.

*Scott, James C. 1990. *Domination and the Arts of Resistance*. New Haven: Yale University Press. *Here and elsewhere Scott has catalogued many forms of resistance by those who cannot mount overt protest without losing their lives.*

Seidman, Gay W. 2007. *Beyond the Boycott*. New York: Russell Sage Foundation.

Sharp, Gene. 2012. *From Dictatorship to Democracy*. New York: New Press.

Silver, Beverly J. 2003. *Forces of Labor*. Cambridge: Cambridge University Press.

*Snow, David A., E. Burke Rochford Jr., Steven K. Worden, and Robert D. Benford. 1986. "Frame Alignment Processes, Micromobilization, and Movement Participation." *American Sociological Review* 51: 464–481. *The article that made frames into the central concept for understanding the cultural dimensions of social movements.*

Snow, David A., Louis A. Zurcher Jr., and Sheldon Ekland-Olson. 1980. "Social Networks and Social Movements." *American Sociological Review* 45: 787–801.

Sobieraj, Sarah. 2011. *Soundbitten*. New York: New York University Press.

Staggenborg, Suzanne, Donna Eder, and Lori Sudderth. 1993. "Women's Culture and Social Change." *Berkeley Journal of Sociology* 38: 31–56.

*Tarrow, Sidney. 1998. *Power in Movement*. Cambridge: Cambridge University Press. *A fine introduction to social movements from a structural perspective. If you can find it, read this lean second edition rather than the recent third edition.*

*Tarrow, Sidney. 2013. *The Language of Contention*. Cambridge: Cambridge University Press. *Words matter.*

References and Suggested Readings

Taylor, Charles. 1989. *Sources of the Self*. Cambridge: Harvard University Press.

*Taylor, Verta. 1996. *Rock-a-by Baby: Feminism, Self-Help, and Postpartum Depression*. New York: Routledge. *How women mobilized to deal with emotions they were not supposed to feel.*

Taylor, Verta, Katrina Kimport, Nella Van Dyke, and Ellen Ann Anderson. 2009. "Culture and Mobilization: Tactical Repertoires, Same-Sex Weddings, and the Impact on Gay Activism." *American Sociological Review* 74: 865–890.

Thörn, Håkan. 2006. *Anti-Apartheid and the Emergence of a Global Civil Society*. New York: Palgrave Macmillan.

Tilly, Charles. 1986. *The Contentious French*. Cambridge: Harvard University Press.

Tilly, Charles. 1995. *Popular Contention in Great Britain*. Cambridge: Harvard University Press.

Tilly, Charles. 2004. *Social Movements, 1768–2004*. Boulder: Paradigm.

*Tilly, Charles. 2008. *Contentious Performances*. Cambridge: Cambridge University Press. *After decades as a structuralist, this historical sociologist increasingly recognized the importance of culture in protest, especially here, in his final book.*

*Touraine, Alain. 1981. *The Voice and the Eye*. Cambridge: Cambridge University Press. *In the 1980s Touraine was the world's dominant scholar of social movements; this book lays out the basics of his approach and still offers many cultural insights.*

*Tucker, Kenneth H., Jr. 2010. *Workers of the World, Enjoy!* Philadelphia: Temple University Press. *Entertaining history of movements that have used and transformed art in the last century.*

Warren, Mark E. 2010. *Fire in the Heart*. New York: Oxford University Press. *Inaugural book in the series "Oxford Studies in Culture and Politics."*

Watts, Edward J. 2010. *Riot in Alexandria*. Berkeley: University of California Press.

Whittier, Nancy. 1995. *Feminist Generations: The Persistence of the Radical Women's Movement*. Philadelphia: Temple University Press.

Whittier, Nancy. 2011. *The Politics of Child Sexual Abuse*. New York: Oxford University Press.

Wood, Elisabeth Jean. 2003. *Insurgent Collective Action and Civil War in El Salvador*. Cambridge: Cambridge University Press.

Young, Michael. 2006. *Bearing Witness Against Sin*. Chicago: University of Chicago Press.

Zolberg, Aristide R. 2008. "Moments of Madness." In *How Many Exceptionalisms?* Philadelphia: Temple University Press.

References and Suggested Readings

Recommended internet sites

http://wagingnonviolence.org/
www.socialmovementstudy.net
www.opendemocracy.net
www.cbsm-asa.org
http://mobilizingideas.wordpress.com/
https://councilforeuropeanstudies.org/research/research-networks/
  social-movements
http://www.interfacejournal.net/
https://portside.org/
http://politicsoutdoors.com/
http://cosmos.eui.eu/Home.aspx

Index

Entries in **bold** refer to the first main occurrence of a key term.

Index

Index

Index

Index